Praise for I C...

Josie has provided a super informative, practical and important text for young athletes. This book is not just key for young athletes, but also extremely useful for sport psychologists working with this population – **Dr Amy Whitehead, School of Sport and Exercise Sciences, Liverpool John Moores University**

The mental aspect of high performance sport is incredibly important & often overlooked. Josie Perry has put together this fantastic resource for young athletes & I'd strongly recommend them to read it and incorporate the many lessons from it. I'd have loved to have had this as a teenager – **Amy Williams MBE, Olympic Champion, Presenter, Speaker, Author, Physical trainer**

Josie has written a must-read primer filled with accessible, practical, and evidence-based techniques for any teenager aspiring to harness their mindset for success – **Dr Andrew Wood, Department of Psychology, Manchester Metropolitan University**

The sport of Triathlon was my passion and my profession for 30 years. For the first half of my career, I worked hard, I was determined to be great, and I felt like I had some ability. But, I struggled with self-doubt and confidence. When I look back at this time, I often wonder how many times I underperformed due to this lack of confidence. "I Can" by Josie Perry is what was missing. This book although written for teenagers, is a brilliant guide for all of us to optimize our performances – **Greg Bennett, Multiple Triathlon World Series Champion, Multiple Olympian, Author, Podcast host - The Greg Bennett Show**

Filled with lessons and mental skills best learned in your teenage years but important to learn at any stage of life, this book is a valuable tool for anyone of any age hoping to achieve high-performance goals in sport - or any other endeavour for that matter – *James Cunnama, Professional Triathlete, South Africa*

The teenage years are when young athletes need to develop a performance lifestyle, a way of life that enables them to perform in all their endeavours, not just their sporting aspirations. A performance-orientated mindset is key component of this. 'I Can' is an invaluable tool for young athletes to develop confidence, conquer their nerves, become braver, learn to deal with setbacks and control their emotions to help them to become successful in whatever they set their mind to – *James Spragg, Cycling Coach, https://www.spraggcyclecoaching.com/*

An insightful and practical approach providing much needed support and understanding for young people. Everything from the language to the layout is thoroughly thought through and very powerful – *Jenny Coady, High Performance Coach Developer, UK Coaching, Performance Coach: West Ham United Women, Former International Basketball Player and Coach.*

This book is a go-to for any teenage athlete who wants to master their mindset. Each chapter presents a superb blend of evidence-based recommendations, engaging practical activities, and inspiring athlete tales; that will equip any teenager to build their personalised mental fitness plan – *Jo Davies, Chartered Sport Psychologist*

As my junior racing career progressed it became glaringly obvious to me that the mind played a vital part in both training and racing. Unlike my physical training which was discussed, progressional and measured, mental training was something that only came up in discussion once I had already become good enough to enter national programs. Aside from a few timely motivational quotes, attached to the top of my workouts, my mental preparation for races was self-taught through trial and error and a natural competitive instinct.

Mental training in sport should not however be limited to 'how to win'. The scope of developing healthily and adaptively to the different challenges and scenarios a life in elite sport can throw at young athletes presents a huge chasm of neglect. This book takes pains to consider that education is a vital tool in any athlete's armoury. Learning its lessons may have helped me considerably through the trials and tribulations that is competitive sport. I could have won more medals, being more satisfied and probably been kinder to myself in general – *Jodie Swallow, Olympian, twice ITU Long Distance World Champion, Ironman 70.3 World Champion, twice Ironman African Champion, and Ironman Asia Pacific Champion*

To unleash sport as more of a force for good in the world, there needs to be far more focus on the mental and emotional aspects of an athlete's journey. This book is wonderfully accessible to younger athletes, with chapters and topics that will resonate with them in their lives both in and out of sport. I have no doubt that it will contribute to readers having an overall more positive experience in sport and also to achieve far more of their potential – *Laurence Halstead, two-time Olympian, Performance Director: Danish Fencing Federation, Director of Mentoring: The True Athlete Project*

This book will provide young athletes the opportunity to reach their full potential. I have played and worked with some of the world's best cricketers and the difference between the world's best and those just outside has always been players 'Mental fitness'. The more young players can understand how they operate mentally, the more chances they will have of being successful – **Lydia Greenway, former England Cricketer, Ashes Winner, World Cup and World T20 Champion, Broadcaster, Author, Head Coach: Oval Invincibles, Founder: www.cricketforgirls.com**

Mental skills are easily overlooked but their impact on performance is huge. This book is an invaluable guide for any young athlete wanting to build their mental toolkit, and practising the suggested exercises is a great way to kickstart success in sport and other areas of life – **Lizzie Simmonds, Double Olympian, Business Coach, Blogger**

Dr Perry combines epic knowledge and brilliant writing skills to offer a book that is deep in its knowledge, but also immensely practical and useful for teenagers and their parents. What excites me most about this book and its resources is that it will give children and their parents the chance to have high impacting conversations about the sports journey. I wish I could write like Josie and will be recommending parents get their kids this book in the sporting pathways which I work – **Richard Shorter – Non-Perfect Dad**

I CAN

I CAN

THE TEENAGE ATHLETE'S
GUIDE TO MENTAL FITNESS

Josephine Perry, PhD

First published in 2021 by Sequoia Books

ISBN
Print: 978-1-914110-00-9
EPUB: 978-1-914110-01-6
MOBI: 978-1-914110-02-3

A CIP record for this book is available from the British Library

Library of Congress Cataloguing-In-Publication Data
Name: Josephine Perry, author
Title: I Can: The Tennage Athlete's Guide to Mental Fitness / Josephine Perry
Description: 1st Edition, Sequoia Books UK 2021
Subjects: LCSH: Adolescent Psychology. Sport Psychology. Sports-Psychological Aspects
Print: 978-1-914110-00-9
EPUB: 978-1-914110-01-6
MOBI: 978-1-914110-02-3

Library of Congress Control Number: 2021926078

Print and Electronic production managed by Deanta Global Publishing Services, Chennai, India

Contents

Acknowledgements

My biggest thank you is always to my husband Paul (who gets the pleasure of numerous drafts to listen to and activities to try out) and my daughter Hattie (who at 4 is already incredibly competitive and loves being active whether it is parkour, swimming, ballet or multi-sport).

Thanks to Andy Peart who came up with the idea of supporting young athletes in this way and for bringing the book and the activities to life.

I would really like to thank all those who gave feedback on drafts: Richard Shorter, Georgia Molloy, Thomas Hill, Jo Dalton, Annie Jonkers and Thomas McGrattan.

My 'success story' athletes have added such insight highlighting what they learnt in their time as elite athletes: Cath Bishop, Dame Sarah Storey, Charlie Hodgson, Joe Weatherly, Shaun Wright-Phillips, Rebecca Adlington, Emma Wiggs, Marilyn Okoro and Richard Kruse.

I am also indebted to the sport psychology researchers who study athletes to help us as applied psychologists support our athletes much better. Researchers such as Karla Drew, Costas Karageorghis, Noel Brick, Amy Whitehead, Samuele Marcora, Andy Lane, Tim Rees, Lew Hardy, Arne Güllich, Bruce Abernethy, Jean Côté, Tim Woodman, Hugh Montgomery and Mustafa Sarkar all produce wonderful studies, a number of which are mentioned in this book.

Finally, and most importantly, thank you to all the junior athletes I have so far worked with. They have trusted their sporting brains to me and taught me as much about how the teenage athlete's mind works as I may have taught them about sport psychology.

Introduction

I can. The mantra of many successful athletes.

Those successful athletes didn't do the hard graft just on the pitch, in the gym, on the track or in the pool. They did the hard graft in their heads too. They learnt that without a raft of mental skills and a performance-focused mindset they have no chance of achieving their sporting dreams.

When they learnt those psychological skills and shaped their mental approach they became successful. They became consistent. They learnt the benefit of showing up to every session, every workout and every competition. They stuck to their plans and used their training, nutrition, strength work and psychology to get the most from themselves. They dedicated time to rest, recover and relax. They learnt to read their bodies and minds and to take those feelings as information, not judgement. They didn't do it alone. They built a team of support around them and valued those people.

This book should help you become one of these athletes. Someone whose body can probably already do lots of the sporting skills but whose brain can now learn to master the mental ones. In here you will learn how your brain works in competition, how to manipulate it to help rather than hinder you and lots of sporting strategies to make the most of that new knowledge. It will stop you from leaving your success to chance.

All the amazing athletes we admire will have had struggles along the way. They may have felt sick with nerves before big competitions, found they didn't put themselves up for selection because their confidence was too low, got knocked back by setback after setback, or lost their temper when things didn't go their way, or they just couldn't stay focused long enough to pick up new skills. No one is immune. They just learnt ways to deal with these issues and cope with the stresses that the pressure of competition can cause.

Without being taught this stuff though we tend to just focus on the physical. It is the go-to place to fix everything. But it is just as important to look after our mental approach and our emotional health. Only when we are physically, mentally and emotionally fit can we become a successful athlete. So, just like you do with your physical practice it is essential that you practice your mental skills and build enough self-awareness so that you can develop an approach which suits you.

> Elite Insight: Michael Phelps (swimming): They say the mental aspect of sports is just as important as the physical part. There can be no doubt about that.

Even if you don't feel like a real 'athlete' right now, you can still benefit. If you compete in a sport and want to be better at it then this book is for you. All the advice is designed for junior athletes who are looking to master their mental skills as much as they are working on their physical ones.

The book is full of questions and activities (over 50 of them) and is not one of those books to keep neat. In fact, I would love you to write all over it, answering the questions, doing the activities and highlighting anything which you'd like to remember. Its power only comes alive when you use it and adapt it to what you need to do to be successful. And the skills we cover will help you not only in your sport but also in school, music and any other hobbies you have; they transfer well into any area of your life.

You can either work through it chapter by chapter (as many of the skills might come in helpful later in life even if you are not struggling with that issue right now) or just pick and choose the chapters which match the issues you are currently facing. Whichever route you choose we'll aim to learn from the best so you can soak up their knowledge and pick up the skills these athletes learnt along the way – think of it as a fast track to mental fitness.

WHY SPORT IS BRILLIANT FOR TEENAGERS

If you ever wonder why you are doing all of this, remember it isn't just for fun, or a future career. The sport you do every day has a wealth of benefits.

As children we do lots of exercise. As we hit our teens that tends to drop. It drops so much that 81% of teenagers do not do as much as the World Health Organization suggests they should, which is an hour a day of activity.

Not doing enough activity is really dangerous as a teen as it is a prime time to become stressed, because of changes going on in our brain as we mature and because of social changes as we find new friends and schools. When we get stressed our bodies get more efficient at storing energy and our obesity risk increases. Obesity increases our risks of acquiring a huge number of diseases, and already over one in six teenagers are obese. The habits we form when we are young tend to stick with us throughout life, so finding a sport you love when you are young and learning how to be brilliant at it will not only reduce obesity risk now but increase your chances of being fit and healthy throughout your whole life.

There are also some immediate benefits of competing in sport as a teen. Health wise you'll have better cardiovascular fitness, healthy cholesterol and stronger bones. Mentally you will have stronger cognitive, communicative and social skills. Helpful for getting great grades and for making lots of friends. In fact, studies show that those who do lots of exercise do better at school. They also develop good life skills like cooperation, self-discipline, coping tactics, competitiveness, leadership and self-confidence. These give you a great platform for a future career, whether that be in sport or anything else. Sport is also great for improving your mental health. Sporting teens have lower levels of stress, depression and anxiety and higher levels of self-esteem, body image and confidence.

The sport you are doing now also puts you in a great place for the rest of your life. A study in Finland tracked a group of 14-year-old athletes and found they were still active 17 years later. A group of teenage girls in Belgium were tracked and found to be playing sports even 20 years later. So, feel proud of yourself for giving yourself such a great start.

> Elite Insight: Rafael Nadal (tennis): The difference between victory and defeat lies not in physical strength or native ability but in having a psychological edge.

WHAT WE WILL LEARN

In Chapter 1 we look at what it takes to be successful. Not to win. But to be successful. There is a big difference, and when you see this difference it can change your whole approach to sport, so you enjoy it much more, and perform better. This approach will help you focus on mastering your sport so you continually improve, can set great goals and appreciate that failure isn't a reflection on you – it is simply an opportunity to learn. We will consider the importance of practice – both your physical skills and your mental ones, not to get perfect, because perfect doesn't exist, but to ensure you continually progress. When you do this you learn much more on how to control the right things in competition so you have the best chance of being successful in your sport.

Chapter 2 looks at how we learn to use the nerves we have before competitions to be excited about the challenge ahead instead of feeling threatened by the risk of failing. It will help you identify your motivation and all the things that might hold you back, like the different stressors we have to deal with in regular life and in competition. We look at how to reduce the number of stressors you have to deal with. We also work on exactly what you can do to get yourself into a challenge mind-set before you go into your competition.

The next chapter is all about how to get braver and push harder in competition. We look at all the tricks you can use to become fearless in your sport and to prepare brilliantly for competition so you are in a great headspace before you start. Many of us have a voice in our head telling us it is fine to be lazy, and this chapter helps us quieten it down by boosting our motivation and using all the tools in our mental toolkit to make everything feel a bit easier.

In Chapter 4 we focus on confidence – how much you have and how you can get more. We look at Gold Standard confidence and all the sources you can use to match your confidence levels to your effort and ability levels.

Emotional control is where a lot of junior athletes struggle, so Chapter 5 helps you become much more in control of your emotions. We will learn how your brain works in competition and discover lots of ways to make it helpful to your performance, not harmful.

Chapter 6 covers concentration and focus. Something we all need to do in our sport but often in very different ways. We will learn how to get better at concentrating when we need to and what interferes with our ability to concentrate. The four different types of focus that we need to use in sport will be dissected, and we will work on how to switch between them quickly. We will finish by looking at the type of distractions you are likely to get and how to manage them.

I have yet to meet an adult athlete who hasn't been injured at least once in their career. Injuries and setbacks happen regularly, and when we learn how to deal with them effectively (as we will in Chapter 7) we can often come back stronger.

In Chapter 8 we look at how we fit in the sports world so it doesn't feel quite so intimidating or lonely. Limiting how much you compare yourself with others and shaping your own culture and climate will make a big difference to your success and your happiness. Creating our own sporting culture with people who are truly on our side is the bonus element that makes searching for success much less stressful and far more fun.

Finally, in Chapter 9 we will look at how to feel like a real athlete. We will follow the idea that when you know your purpose and have passion that you are able to ace your performance. Where your motivation comes from and what you see as your values will give you a great framework, and then becoming an expert in yourself through understanding your perceptions, your personality and your preferences will give you a comfortable foundation to develop as an athlete. When you add onto this positive wellbeing you will be in a great place to feel, think and behave like a successful athlete.

In each chapter there will be questions to think about and answer, activities to complete, elite insights from some of the best athletes in the world and interviews with highly successful athletes who will bring each approach to life and show how the tools and approaches you are learning made them really successful in their sport.

The book isn't referenced as I hope this makes it easier to use; however, there is a 'further reading' section at the end which will highlight where you can find extra resources or learn more about the athletes quoted.

So, now you know what to expect, here is your first task.

Question: What would I like to be able to do better after reading this book?

1.

2.

3.

To help you make a start on those improvements there is one tool that can make a big difference in how well you put your intentions into reality and how well you develop a great mental approach to your sport. It will help you develop robust confidence and remind you that you have the skills you need and that you've put the effort in to master them. It becomes key to remembering what you have achieved (the outcomes and the improvements). It is a training diary.

Activity: Set up your training diary

To do our training diary we have to go old school. No tech. A paper diary is the best thing to use because studies have found that physically writing things down helps speed up our skill and knowledge acquisition. Filling it in every day means that we have tonnes of information to help us track how we are doing against our goals; prepare well for competition; build our gratitude levels; have some space to reflect on our sport; notice our strengths and weaknesses; spot patterns of behaviour, illness or injury and build our confidence.

> Elite Insight: Mo Farah (running): A training diary can really help to keep you motivated and I'd recommend everyone keep some sort of running log. Like everyone, I have moments of self-doubt and there's nothing better than flicking back to see how well you have been running.

We look to log:

1. Physical training including drills
2. Fitness or strength and conditioning sessions
3. Physical or mental skills we worked on
4. Any niggles or injuries
5. Any particularly strong (good or bad) feelings around our sport

For important training sessions or competition days, we can also add in:

1. My fitness levels seem ...
2. The skill I mastered best was ...
3. What I did well in this session ...
4. The negative thoughts I had were ...
5. What I have gained by doing this session?

Longer term, maybe weekly or monthly we can also think about adding some notes:

1. The obstacles I am currently facing are ...
2. The three strengths I have that I value the most are ...
3. What could I change in my environment to help me succeed?
4. When it gets hard I need to remember ...

If you struggle to fill it in, try to do it at the same time each day so it becomes a habit.

An example training diary for a 15-year-old cross-country runner:

Mon 1st	3-mile run with dad. Felt nice and easy. Chatted. 30 minutes. Basic stretches when got home Chatted about approach to races while running – felt helpful. Going to try his breathing technique before next race. No niggles. Legs feeling bouncy.
Tues 2nd	Rest day Practised imagery to boost mental skills Felt a bit guilty for not running – I know I shouldn't feel guilty. Rest is important to get stronger.
Wed 3rd	School cross-country club. Long warm-up, lots of drills, found the high knees tricky, must stretch more, then a group run. Enjoyed running with the others. Don't like running alone.
Thur 4th	45-minute football match in PE today. Felt good practice for the twists and changes of direction we have in cross-country. Feels like getting good endurance. Practised sprinting drills in the park with Jamie after school (about 30 minutes). Jamie is much better than me – makes me want to work harder – will use it as a prompt not to get lazy in sessions.

Your training diary becomes really helpful just before competition as you will be able to look back and see how you have managed difficult situations in the past, how you managed sessions you never thought you could, spot the strengths you have developed and notice how much effort you have been investing in your goals. All of these help build your competition confidence and improve your overall sporting success.

CHAPTER 1

I can be successful

There is a quote thrown around sport – painted on the walls of gyms, flagged up in sports books, printed onto t-shirts – that says "winning isn't everything, it's the only thing." I disagree. Winning is fun. It is exciting. It is awesome. For a moment. But then it is gone. Success, whatever you choose your version of success to be, is far more important in sport. When you focus on success you can be proud of being an athlete.

When young kids are asked why they play their sport the number one answer is always 'to have fun'. And yet we hit a certain age and the sport we once loved to play because we got to enjoy ourselves, be with our friends, learn new skills or feel fit and healthy gets taken over by something that previously hadn't even made the top ten of reasons to play: To win.

When the fun starts to go and is replaced by this focus on winning a huge number (some studies suggest 85%) of young athletes drop out of sport. Yet where does this focus on winning come from? It doesn't seem to be from teens themselves. As researchers found, teenagers would rather get to play on a losing team than sit on the bench for a winning one.

Winning isn't why your parents want you to play either. They love that sports help you learn moral principles, team work and ways to bounce back from disappointments, that they help you make great friends and mix with a wide range of people and they feel comforted knowing they keep you fit and healthy and boost your confidence.

Coaches certainly want to feel they have taught their athletes well, and they want to coach successful, happy athletes. But most go into coaching because they love the sport they coach and want to bring that joy to more people. So why does everything feel focused on winning when what we actually want to feel is successful?

WINNING VERSUS SUCCESS

The trouble is, winning is so easy to measure. It is black and white. Did you win or did you lose? Success is far more subtle. And it is personal. Success to me may feel like failure to you. And vice versa. But, while everything seems focused on winning or not, success matters far more because winning is judged by others. Success can be judged by ourselves. And if we want to be happy in life we need to focus on measuring our lives by what matters to us and whether we achieve it – not on what matters to others and measuring ourselves by them. That route only leads to misery.

> Elite Insight: Joe Weatherly (cricket): I have a passion for Cricket but I think what is deeper routed is just a passion to get better to achieve my potential in something. Cricket is my medium but if I wasn't a cricketer I think I would be relentlessly pursuing something else and just every day trying to get better at it. My motivation is to be the best I can be and to maximise my potential in cricket.

We will talk a lot about success in this book. And ways to achieve it. But it is important to remember that success doesn't immediately mean winning. Success is whatever you choose it to be. It will be different for each of us. It might well look like a big shiny medal, or a trophy, or our name in the local paper talking about our achievements; all of those are great. But it might also be having a brilliant social life through our sport, lots of trips around the country to competitions or feeling fit and healthy enough to take on any sport that appeals. Whatever our version of success, we will only get it if we stop focusing on winning and instead develop our sporting mastery. And that is what we will do in every chapter.

Question: I see success in my sport as ...

MASTERING MASTERY

When we focus on winning, our attention goes on outcomes and results and other people. Having a focus here is really unhelpful because it actually increases our chances of losing. Instead, when we focus on mastering our sport, skills, fitness and decision-making, we win more often. Mastering our sport requires us to work on developing excellence.

We develop excellence by purposefully working on it. We make it our goal, and we break down what excellence means to us. Now you know what you see success as you can split it up into all the elements of excellence we will need to work on to achieve it.

To achieve excellence we need to understand the barriers that are currently stopping us. Are we too busy with other things? Are we not focused enough in training? Would we rather be hanging out with friends? Is our rubbish diet causing lots of illness? Whatever the barriers are, they need to be acknowledged and turned into actionable, focused plans. One way to do this is through a performance profile.

Activity: Performance profile

Look back to your answer on what you would see as success in your sport and write it down in the top left-hand box.

Then think of eight elements which you will need to focus on to achieve your version of success. If you struggle perhaps take two from each of these areas:

- Lifestyle and support
- Technical and tactical skills
- Physical preparation and fitness
- Mental approaches and behaviours.

If you still have a few sections unfilled, research someone you know – personally, in your sport or even a famous athlete to see what they have done to get the type of success you would like for yourself.

To achieve success I need to do ...	If 1 was never and 5 was always I would currently score myself ...

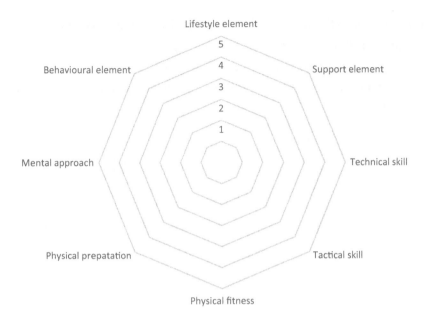

For example, a soccer player who wanted to be good enough to play in her team's local derby created a performance profile which looked like this:

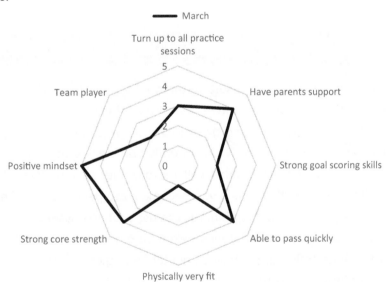

The more space inside your diagram the closer you are to your ideal level of success. It shows this soccer player that, in order to have a chance of making it onto the team, she needs to work on her fitness, practise goal shooting and become more of a team player.

Do you have lots of space in your diagram?

What are the three biggest things your diagram highlights you need to work on?

1.

2.

3.

You can come back to this every few months and check out where you are improving.

SETTING MASTERY-FOCUSED GOALS

We can focus on mastery by setting the right type of goals. Goals turn your intentions into actions and set a clear direction for where you want to go with your sport. Setting goals in a structured way can help you change any behaviours which are currently holding you back and help you to focus on all the ways that will improve your performance. They will influence your efforts, help you become more persistent and keep you focused in the right direction. You can use your goal setting to make sure you have thought about every element required to succeed. This could include training, practising mental strategies, travel, strength, conditioning and nutrition.

By creating your performance profile you have already started set-ting some goals. These will all be goals within your control that you get to work on to become excellent in your sport.

Elite Insight: Michael Phelps (swimming): Every year since I have been swimming competitively I have set goals for myself. In writing. The goal sheet was mandatory. I got used to it and it became a habit. … I didn't look at the sheet every day. I pretty much memorized it, how fast I wanted to swim and what I had to do to get there.

We set three layers of goals. The first layer is an outcome goal. You can only have one (if we have two then we are less likely to achieve either) and it is often something around competition. It may involve a result, a place in the rankings or a qualification spot. It doesn't have to though. They could involve competing in new places (qualifying for an overseas competition), using sport as a way of helping others (fundraising) or developing a really difficult skill. These outcome goals will often involve other people, so will be really motivating but not that controllable.

Next, we have performance goals. These are the things which show us if we are likely to reach our outcome. They are much more controllable because they just focus on us, no one else. It might be a personal best time, a distance to hit, a score to obtain or an ability to play a certain way. Our performances feed into the outcomes, so if we achieve our performance goals we would be likely to achieve our outcome goal too. But even if we don't, we will still have mastered much more of our sport.

Finally, we have our process goals. These are drawn from our performance goals and specify the behaviours, actions, strategies and tactics we need to have in training or competition if we are to make our performance goal happen. For a fencer this might be practising staying patient on the piste, or for a runner it might be completing a long, slow run each week. Repeating these actions over and over again stops them from being choices and makes them habits. And when you see how often you are achieving your process goals you get lots of reasons to celebrate.

Activity: Set your goals

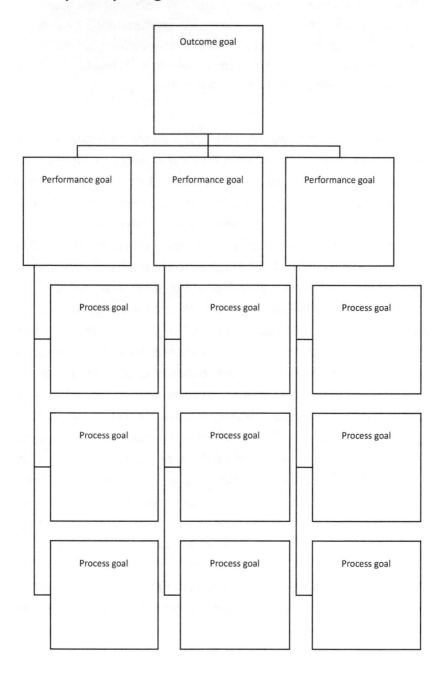

SCALE YOUR GOALS UP

Once you have set your goals look back over them and to make them really work for you then make sure they are SCALED UP.

- Specific – so you know exactly what you are aiming for – to the point where you can visualise what it will look and feel like to achieve it.
- Clear – so you are not tempted to change them when it gets hard.
- Achievable – If we set our goals too high we will get disappointed and disillusioned. Too low and we won't be bothered to put in any effort.
- Layered – When we focus only on outcome we develop unrealistic future expectations, which reduce our confidence, increase anxiety, stop us from putting so much effort in and cause poor performance. It is the performance and process goals which help us develop more realistic expectations. Having this mixture of three types of goals means we can focus on the right things: our effort levels, our persistence and our strategies for success.
- Exciting – When you think about the outcome goal it needs to make your tummy flip with excitement.
- Deadline – Sometimes life gets in the way of our sport; deadlines help us stay on track.
- U – Focus as much as possible on things you personally can control.
- Positive – Focus on what you are trying to achieve – not on what you want to avoid.

When you work on your goals in this way you will eventually get to a point when your current milestones turn into your new steppingstones and you can see how far you have progressed.

STAYING GOAL DRIVEN

To be a really successful athlete you need to make goal setting a key part of your sport. You might already do it at the start of a season, but if you set mini goals for each practice session you should get much better at mastering individual skills or attitudes and finish every training session with a buzz of success. These small goals won't be around outcomes but around ways you would like to perform.

Examples from a range of sports could be:

- I want to feel relaxed when I play today
- I want to behave like a professional
- I will do my performance routine before every shot
- I will focus on reframing unhelpful thoughts
- I will spend time in the breaks reflecting on whether I am happy with each key decision
- I will do my breathing exercise while walking to my ball
- I will practise pushing harder when I feel tired
- I will focus on showing amazing technique.

DON'T RUSH

If you are driven and determined and love your sport it is natural for you to want to be really good at it as soon as you can. But you do have time to slow down and enjoy your sport more. Studies have shown that many of those who do well as seniors weren't on the radar when they were much younger and those who do really well as juniors don't go on to make it so as seniors. In fact, the younger an athlete starts to take their sport seriously, the shorter their career in that sport is likely to be. Those who spend more of their childhood playing lots of different sports and wait until they are around 13 or 14 before specialising in just one tend to do best as seniors. This time to learn lots of different skills in lots of different sports gives them lots of advantages.

Researchers found that the average age athletes tend to win medals across the 57 Olympic events is 26. So if you are in your teens now you still have a long time to get there – and that time needs to be focused on learning to master the key skills, on showing gradual improvement and learning how to be successful in your sport. Focusing on the process now will pay you back many times over in the long term.

You don't even need to specialise by 14. Data from elite athletes in the UK found that those who came into a sport through talent transfer programmes (where someone is considered athletically talented but unlikely to reach the top in their current sport) between the ages of 16 and 25 will be able to reach the same level as longer-term athletes in their sport within a year.

You don't need to be in an academy or talent system either. In countries where they have elite sports schools (such as Germany and the Netherlands) there is no difference in success levels between those who attended one of these schools and those who didn't. And those who didn't attend the sports school got better academic outcomes in addition to being just as good in their sport.

A few athletes make their mark as teenagers and carry on to achieve great things. Usain Bolt was World Junior 200-metre champion when he was 16. He maintained that dominance. But many others never live up to the hype they received in their teens. Injury, illness, reduced motivation, poor coaching, rubbish facilities or being unable at access funding all impact how well someone is likely to do as a senior athlete. In fact, when researcher Karla Drew investigated the numbers she found that 63% of athletes who competed for Britain at the World Junior Champs never improved on their PB at senior level and 67% never represented their country as an adult either. She found that the ones who do make it are those who develop competition coping strategies, have lots of sport-specific knowledge, clearly define goals, learn from going to championships and are able to achieve a life-sport balance. These are all things you will develop in this book. The athletes who are too focused on being an athlete to the detriment of everything else tend not to make it.

There are a few sports, like gymnastics and swimming, that can be excluded from this as athletes become elites very young and specialise and focus on deliberate practice earlier. However, it is also good to know that the average age of Olympic medallists in these sports is rising, so athletes in these sports will soon get more time to grow into them too.

Finally, our abilities in some sports will be impacted by our body shape and size. In general, rugby players are muscular, gymnasts are flexible and powerful, basketball players are tall and swimmers often have big hands and feet. But size isn't everything. And we all mature and develop at different stages, so although you might have been very good at certain sports when you were young you may not suit that sport after puberty. If you love playing sport and doing well against others, rather than enjoying a specific sport for the love of it, then keeping going with lots of different sports leaves the door open to find a sport which works for your body type, increasing your chances of success.

A way to help us see the long-term perspective needed to succeed in sport is to study how others have done it. Seeing other athletes work hard and succeed can be really motivational. It is especially motivational if we relate to them in some way. Once they achieve something then we realise perhaps we could too. Think about what happened when Roger Bannister broke the 4-minute mile in 1954 and Kathrine Switzer ran the Boston Marathon in 1967. For years everyone thought neither were possible and yet, as soon as Bannister broke the mile time, 12 other runners managed to break the same 'impossible' barrier that year. When Switzer showed that women were perfectly capable of running 26.2 miles it encouraged millions of others to do the same. We all have our own barriers, so finding people that have crossed similar hurdles and copying their behaviours can help us find our own version of success.

Activity: Mentor magic

The athletes I really admire:

Name: Why:

Name: Why:

Name: Why:

What behaviours or attitudes I can take from them and use in my own sport:

Behaviour / Attitude 1:

Behaviour / Attitude 2:

Behaviour / Attitude 3:

FOLLOWING A WIN OR LEARN APPROACH

When we have a long-term plan for our sport and are focused on mastering it to the best of our abilities we won't get so hung up about winning or losing. But we will get hung up about improving. Focusing on improving stops us from being so afraid to lose. And losing actually helps us improve because failure is a form of feedback. Losing becomes an important part of our journey to be a better athlete; as we end up learning far more from the competitions that go wrong than the ones we win, we can use them to develop a 'win or learn approach'.

Elite Insight: Tanni Grey-Thompson (wheelchair racer): I learnt a lot from not winning. We used to spend lots of time evaluating races, looking at the good, the bad, the improvements and what I could have done differently. ... You can't go backwards. You have to learn from it and do something different next time.

To bring this approach to life you need to get into the habit of analysing competitions. This helps you understand how to improve future performances, develop better tactics and consider how you cope under pressure; it also ensures you don't forget about the things you are really good at. The analysis makes you more self-aware so you learn what does and doesn't work for you.

Activity: Post competition analysis

Complete this analysis the day after a competition. If you do it straight after it will be too full of emotion.

To fill in your top boxes think about:

- Physical fitness and conditioning
- Skills used
- Tactics used
- Preparation
- Logistics
- Equipment
- Nutrition
- Mental approach and focus.

And always follow the two rules:

1. Have as many points in the 'what went well' as the 'what could have gone better' box. We want you to have a balanced analysis.
2. Once you have finished circle two things in the bottom boxes which will become your focus for the next few weeks – think of them as your action plan.

What went well	Would have gone better if ...
1.	1.
2.	2.
3.	3.
Will keep doing	**Will change**

If you keep all your post-competition analysis sheets you can look back over them at the start of each new season to spot any patterns. This will help you set your goals for the next year.

PRACTICE MAKES PROGRESS

You have probably heard the phrase 'practice makes perfect'. It is usually repeated by people who want us to get so good at something that we can do it without thinking. The intention is good, and it can make us excellent in our sporting techniques. But it is a risky approach because it celebrates perfectionism, and perfectionism can make you totally and utterly miserable.

Perfectionism is a personality trait, something that is within us, and so drives the way we approach tasks or goals. Having it means we constantly strive to do everything flawlessly, to exceptionally high standards and when we don't achieve them (because perfection is impossible to achieve) we feel like a failure.

So, what are the upsides? Perfectionists can be really motivated, very conscientious, follow processes and work really hard. They set themselves high targets and do whatever it takes to meet them. We would assume that would be a great way to ensure sporting success. But it also has down sides. Big ones. One of the big issues is that while it might make us work hard in training and practice, when we get into competition there are just too many uncontrollables for everything to ever go as well as a perfectionist would want. In competition, if we start over-thinking, worrying about our technique or skills and overanalysing our performance uses up loads of our mental energy and we start berating ourselves over what we have just failed at rather than staying in the moment and focusing on what we need to do right now.

> Elite Insight: Richard Kruse (fencer): I was a perfectionist so I was never exactly happy. When you are competing you are never really happy with what you have done. That is the irony of being an athlete. You always want more. You are greedy. You are always looking for that extra thing. I saw a slogan once in some gym saying 'Elite level athletes, they chase perfection. They never get there but in the process they achieve excellence.' I think that explains it well.

More importantly if you don't want to be just an average athlete – but an exceptional one – you'll need to take risks. As a perfectionist risk-taking can be tricky as you might feel worried about making mistakes as they will feel very personal – like you have a flaw. This can feel extra tricky when you are in a team sport as you might feel pressure to perform well and keen not to let anyone down. It means you might play more defensively and actually, unintentionally, perform worse.

When we are perfectionistic we often like to have numbers or measurable achievements to focus on. These can make us fixated on small elements and forget about the big picture. There will often be times that a competition can feel like it is going badly – a poor height in pole vault, a slow swim time in a triathlon or a missed shot in golf, but there are often really good reasons for this which we don't realise at the time – a gust of wind in the pole vault, a very strong current in the triathlon or a broken club in golf. Beating ourselves up for not going perfectly only causes us harm and writes off a competition where we were actually going really well.

Beyond this, far more important than success in sport is our mental health in life. And perfectionists can struggle with their mental health as they are pursuing the unobtainable. A number of studies have found that perfectionists are more likely to suffer from illnesses like depression, anxiety and burnout. When we start out doing a sport one of the best things is that it gives us space away from stress, giving us a way to cope with things like schoolwork or troubles with friends or at home. If we get good at it then we start to expect certain levels of achievement from ourselves. This means instead of it being a brilliant stress reliever our sport becomes an additional pressure and can suck away lots of the joy.

Perfectionists are also at a higher risk of eating disorders. These aren't just the disorders we know lots about, like anorexia, but also disordered eating which is thought to be more common like RED-S (relative energy deficiency in sport) where we don't purposely lose weight, but we are exercising a lot and don't fuel that exercise well enough. It can cause harm to our hormones, make us exhausted and burnt out, and increases risks of bone fractures; girls may lose their periods now and may strug-gle with fertility problems when they get older.

There is also one final downside to being a perfectionist in sport – because perfection isn't possible, we will continually feel like a failure. You may have worked really hard, achieved amazing results, mastered new skills and tactics and outmanoeuvred your rivals but you still won't be satisfied. Your inner bully will be telling you that none of that was good enough. You'll be picking over every single mistake and beating yourself up. That is no way to enjoy your sport – or your life.

ADAPTING PERFECTIONISM

If you think you might be perfectionistic consider how you can use it to your advantage to get really good at your sport but also how you can protect yourself from the down sides.

Using it to your advantage	Minimising the negative
Break things down into small elements so you can do deliberate practice to nail every skill	Focus on practice and process rather than achieving the 'perfect outcome'
Focus on the effort you have put in (rather than on all the extra things you wish you had done)	Practise 'problem-focused coping' where you don't think about the result but consider what was actually going on, identify if your perfectionism held you back and pick a different solution to try next time
Give yourself goals in competition that focus on taking risks and leaving your comfort zone	Chat to someone about the pressures you feel in competition so you share the stress and get more perspective

Adaptive perfectionism is where you focus on striving to achieve very high standards but are able to keep your sport and sporting outcomes in perspective. It is a strong place to be. If you can get to this level you can do very well. One technique to develop this is to master the individual skills you need for your sporting success. This makes you focus on the processes and gives you great confidence that when you need the skills you are an expert at using them.

Activity: Skills sheet

A skills sheet helps us to track what we are focusing on so we keep working until we have covered everything we need to. Just the process of creating it helps you to identify the skills you need to master to achieve your goal, and the need to fill it in means you do regular practice to give you the best chance at doing well.

When you have filled it in you have a sheet of evidence to read through to remind you of all the skills you have mastered, and this should help you feel more confident and focused on using them to perform brilliantly.

The skills should be those which, once mastered, will help you step up your performance levels. Some of these may already be in your mind. If you struggle to identify more read through your performance profile, look at the process goals you developed and look at what you admired in your role models. These should give you some ideas of what to add into your skills sheet. List them in the left-hand column.

Each time you nail that skill in training or competition write the date in the box. When you have completed the sheet you will have evidence that on 50 separate occasions you have shown mastery of your sport.

Skill	Date	Date	Date	Date	Date

CONTROL JUST THE CONTROLLABLES

There are lots of things that influence how successful we are likely to be in our sport. A lot of them we have absolutely no control over whatsoever. It is really frustrating. But if there is nothing we can influence it is better for our mental health and levels of happiness to put these things to one side, and instead just focus on the stuff we can change.

There are five things which influence our success that we have no control over:

- Our parents. They have two huge influences on whether we are likely to be successful in our sport. Their genes are incredibly important. Genetic factors have been found to explain up to 80% of our key sporting elements like body mass, explosive strength, speed, reaction time, flexibility, balance and VO_2max. Some genes even influence whether you are likely to participate in sport. How much money your parents have as you grow up is also important as some sports will feel inaccessible if you are on a low income or at a school where that sport is not played.

- When in the year we are born. Researchers who looked at 58 studies covering the birthdays of athletes found those born earlier in their country's school year do best. They will be stronger so do better early on and are then likely to get picked for teams so get more practice, increasing their development. Those who are not so strong early on might drop out or not take up that sport in the first place as they expect to be worse.

- Our personality. Personality can have some impact with more successful athletes having higher levels of conscientiousness, optimism and hope, more use of adaptive perfectionism, being competitive and proactive.

- Where we grow up. When researchers studied the backgrounds of elite athletes on the GB Olympic pathway programmes they found that they were most likely to have been born in a small town of between 50,000 and 100,000 people and attend primary and high school in a small village. This might well be because of the type and closeness to relevant sporting facilities that you would have in towns of this size.

- Our experience of trauma. Studies have found that if we experience some kind of emotional trauma in childhood, such as our parents getting divorced, being injured, suffering a bereavement or having our schooling disrupted, it can help us develop key mental strengths like grit or resilience and teach us some good ways to cope with stress.

Elite Insight: Jason Kenny (cycling): There was luck involved. The country had just one Olympic-standard velodrome at that point, and it just happened to be fifteen miles from our house. Had I been bought up in Newcastle, Leeds, Birmingham or Bristol there would have been no indoor cycling and no Olympic gold medals.

As we can't change our parents, our date of birth or where we grow up and we do not want trauma just to be better at sport we need to focus on the areas we all have the power to influence. These six areas are where we can put all our efforts.

- Practice efforts. One of the most important elements is the practice and training we put in. The million-dollar question is, how much? Studies on chess players and violinists suggest that it took those performers 10,000 hours or 10 years of practice to achieve their 'expert' status. While this study is regularly quoted in sports books and magazines it isn't right for athletes. Studies looking specifically at athletes suggests that to move from novice to elite (representing your country as a senior) can take around 7.5 years. A number of studies in team sports have found that you can reach international level in fewer than 5000 hours if the practice you do in those hours is very deliberate – more focused on the skills, moves and decisions you need to make in your sport. When you are really young though it is less about deliberate learning and more about having fun. The athletes who don't take it too seriously too young are those who tend to excel.

- Support. Another key element of success involves surrounding yourself with the right people. Your family, friends, coaches and support staff are really important to your success if you are to become an elite athlete. Of course they bring technical skills that help you physically perform better and logistical support to get you to training and competitions, but they can also help you develop psychological skills and mental flexibility and provide a supportive environment for you to develop.

- Culture. The culture of the team or sport you are in is also important. Being able to make mistakes without negative consequences is vital. Being able to feel like yourself means you enjoy training much more so you are more likely to show up. If you turn up to training and there are no nerves about how you might be treated or whether a coach will yell at you or if the favourites will get all the focus again you are much more likely to thrive.

- Recovery. How you prioritise recovery, rest and sleep are key. We don't get stronger when we train. We get stronger when we recover from the training. Too little rest and recovery and we are likely to end up injured. Good quality rest, recovery and sleep and we will feel good and perform excellently.

- Emotional control. Another key area of importance that you have lots of control over is how well you control your emotions. If you are throwing your racquet across a tennis court in frustration or sulking every time you miss a penalty you'll be unpopular with your teammates and easier to beat. Get in control of these elements and your opportunities will increase. We'll work on this in Chapter 5.

- Mental skills. Successful athletes have higher levels of motivation, confidence, perceived control, mental toughness and resilience, are better at coping with adversity and high-pressure situations, use anxiety to enhance performance and use lots of mental skills. Helpfully, these are all characteristics and skills you can work on, and are exactly what we will cover in this book.

Controllable elements of success

For athletes:

Diligence about training
Surrounding ourselves with the right people
Our attitude
Our effort levels in training and competition
The physical and mental skills we focus on
The way we communicate

For teams:

A feeling of all being in it together
Specific roles for each member
Structured ways of communicating
A culture-giving (sometimes unofficial) rules about how to behave
A joint goal
Support for each other

SUCCESS STORY: CATH BISHOP

Cath Bishop won two world championships in rowing (both on the water and indoors) and went to three Olympic Games. She didn't rush her sporting career as she only started rowing when she was 18. She competed at the Atlanta Olympics only 6 years later. She raced again in the Sydney Olympics and won an Olympic silver medal in Athens when she raced in the pair with Katherine Grainger. Here she tells us all about what made her successful.

When we talk about winning verses success, I think success for me is a much bigger, broader concept. Winning is just one way you might be successful. Success will consist of lots of different criteria; the way you approach something, the way you connect, the way you work within a team and the way that you learn from it. Success has many prongs to it and you really build those up to make sure winning is just one of many things. Winning is a milestone but is not the endpoint. It is just a means to other things; to discovering, to exploring where you might be able to go with your potential. Crossing the finish line first doesn't mean anything if you don't connect it with anything afterwards. Getting a medal or crossing the line is just a moment in time but what is important is what you take from that.

Winning doesn't need to be about someone else losing. Winning can also be about you doing your best, providing your best performance. That is when we master mastery. Success can be about exploring your potential, with other people. When you focus on beating someone else you put a limit on what is possible and you become defined by somebody else. How will hating my opponent make me go faster? It should be much more about exploring our own untapped potential.

I wasn't very successful at sport at school. We didn't have the big variety of sports we now have so I did some hockey and netball but didn't make the teams. I loved the drama of the Olympics but I never expected to go there. At 18 when I went to university some friends started rowing but I didn't plan to because you had to get up early and it looked like really hard work. They persuaded me to give it a go. I very nearly didn't because in my head I had voices saying 'you'll look stupid, you won't be very good, you're not sporty, don't do it' but there was also another voice saying: what have you got to lose, why don't you give it a go, you'd like to try it wouldn't you.' There was absolutely zero expectation of me doing anything so I purely fell in love with the sport and I am so grateful I had that opportunity.

I was with friends; laughing, collaborating and I loved the experience of being in the boat. After nine months people were saying you are quite good and I should try rowing at the next level. I always had a sense of how to improve to progress to that next level so I had a great improvement curve but I didn't have a fixed sense of what was at the top. It was always about small steps rather than any massive leap, almost like a ladder that's going up into the cloud. I didn't know the rungs on that ladder were leading to the Olympics. After four years my coach said you have potential and if you train pretty much full time the next level is getting into the British team. The process was good so I never had to deal with expectation, the Olympics rung was just too far away, so I could focus on just what I needed to do at each level.

The more I focused on the moment the better I performed. In rowing, the 2,000 metre line feels so far away the less you think about it the better. I just need to focus on what is happening with the boat and the adjustments I need to make in the next stroke. I can't think about the stroke in 50 strokes time because I'll be in a completely different part of the lake. It is all about focusing on the stroke I am on and how do I build on that to make the next one better. Thinking about what happens if we win or if we lose was just wasted energy and that doesn't make the boat go faster. In fact, every time I thought 'I have got to win' it did nothing to help and probably brought a tension that hindered me.

Our approach was 'whether we win or lose we are going to look and see what we can learn and improve for next time'. This took off the shackles of expectation so we could do our best and then think about where we go next. This learning approach is part of your mindset and worked because our mindset is the element that we have most control over. The approach you bring, your attitude, the responses you choose to take. You need to invest in that and to use your mind not just to drive you on but to review, to reflect, to look after yourself.

CHAPTER 2

I can handle my nerves

We can talk the talk and say we want to do well but what matters is how much, and why. How much are you willing to invest in your sport to succeed? Why do you want to succeed?

Doing well, taking the effort to rock up to practise sessions requires us to be motivated. Motivation is crucial for success. It is our ability to start something, and keep going, despite everything that tries to throw us off course along the way. It is our internal fire which sets the direction and intensity of the effort we put into our sport. Without our desire being lit and constantly fuelled all our other physical and mental skills become redundant. We struggle to achieve anything. But when that fire is stoked, we will go above and beyond to put in the effort that will bring us success. In sport, motivation is really important as it is something we completely control. Being in control makes all the difference to feeling confident. Instead of our sporting events feeling like a threat, motivation and control help us feel like they will be an exciting challenge.

For anyone to feel any type of motivation we need to have five clear things in place: a goal that makes us super-excited, to be good at the skills required to achieve that goal, to feel like we belong in our sport and with the people in it, to have control over our own choices in sport and to actually enjoy doing it. If we are lacking in motivation the first step is to find out where – to see exactly which element is missing.

Activity: Motivation matters

Tick the boxes which match where you feel you are right now

1. I have a goal I am excited about ☐
2. I feel like I belong in my sport ☐
3. I have the skills that are required to do well in my sport ☐
4. I get to choose my own direction in my sport ☐
5. I enjoy doing my sport ☐

If you have ticked all the boxes then fantastic. If any don't ring true with you right now get thinking about how you can change things. If your goal doesn't twist your tummy with excitement you need to find a new one which does. If you don't feel like you belong in your sport, figure out why. Is it the other athletes, the culture, the environment, the coaches? Is it possible to change how you react to them or to find a different team or place to train? If you haven't got the skills you need then it is time to get your head down and build them. The 'Skills Sheet' in Chapter 1 can help with this. If you don't get to choose your own direction then question who is and you might be able to wrestle some power back.

When we are truly motivated and have ticked all the boxes above we have nothing holding us back. Right? Afraid not. We can absolutely want to succeed and have lots of great things in place to help us but still find we are coming up against barriers. The biggest barriers are injury (we'll come back to this in Chapter 7) and stress.

STRIP OUT YOUR STRESSORS

We all experience stress. In everyday life and in our sport. How well we can cope with the stress has a big influence on our success. We get stressed when we don't feel like we are able to cope with the stressors (the individual things which worry or annoy us) in front of us. The stress comes when we feel like there is a big imbalance between the demands on us (our stressors) and our abilities to meet them. When the demands have big consequences, or we have lots of them, our stress levels rise and we are likely to get anxious.

There are millions of stressors. They are the things which cause tension in our lives. They can come from sport (competitions, coaches, pressure), school (coursework, teachers, homework, exams), home (chores, caring, brothers and sisters, parents) and social life (other teens, bullying, tech, clothes, allowances, etc.). It isn't the stressors themselves which are the problem though – if we are in a good place mentally, feel strong, supported and confident then we could have lots of stressors but no stress. It is whether we feel we have the right resources in place to manage the stressors that impacts how much stress it will cause us.

What causes us stress is completely personal. You may feel completely relaxed taking a penalty as you have taken hundreds before and you know you rarely miss. A teammate may see penalty-taking as terrifying as they have no experience and few skills. This would cause them a huge amount of stress as the demands feel high and their ability to meet them is low.

The more stressors we come up against and the fewer coping mechanisms we have the more we will feel stressed. There may be some big stressors that cause everyone tough times – exams, moving house, changing school – but most of the time we are dealing with lots of small but annoying hassles which, if we don't have a handle on them, can make us feel tense, grumpy and out of sorts. If there are too many they can start to impact our training and the way we perform in competition.

> Elite Insight: Alistair Brownlee (triathlon): The pressure was suddenly crushing me. I looked around and thought wow – not only does everyone expect me to win, they think winning is an inevitable outcome.

A study in 2012 looked at the stressors athletes might have to deal with and identified 339 of them. On top of those general sports stressors you will also have those which relate to your own home, school and social situations. There are three main types of stressors for junior athletes: competitive, organisational and personal.

- Competitive: The stressors that come because you have entered a competition or are giving some type of performance.

- Organisational: The stressors that come from being part of a sporting organisation. This might be a team, a club or a governing body of the sport. They usually depend on your sport and your level. One study actually identified 640 distinct organisational stressors for athletes, and the research suggests this organisational area is where the biggest stresses come from when you are competing at a high level.

- Personal: These are the stressors we all come across at one point or another in life – whether or not we do sport.

Activity: Identify your stressors and stresses

Look through the list below of 50 of the most common stressors that athletes have to deal with and tick all those which effect you. Add a second tick if you also find that stressor is really stressing you out. Where you have two ticks you can start to think about what you can do to better handle that stressor. Sometimes we don't even need to try to fix it – just being aware that something triggers us means we can be more controlled in dealing with it.

1.	Physical preparation for competition		
2.	Mental preparation for competition		
3.	Technical preparation for competition		
4.	Tactical preparation for competition		
5.	Pain of injury		
6.	Fear of getting injured		

7.	Frustration of injury and having to miss out on things		
8.	Pressure to perform		
9.	Making mistakes during competition		
10.	Not making progress or achieving goals		
11.	Performing poorly		
12.	Not performing the way I or others expect me to		
13.	Keeping or improving my ranking		
14.	Being the favourite for a competition		
15.	Expectations from myself		
16.	Expectations from others		
17.	Having to perform in front of others		
18.	Judgement and feedback from coaches		
19.	Judgement from teammates		
20.	Worries about letting other people down		
21.	Not being recognised for achievements		
22.	Competing against better athletes		
23.	Competing against athletes I should beat		
24.	Competitors being devious or cheating		
25.	Unfairness from umpire or referee		
26.	Coach's behaviour or attitude		
27.	Coach's personality or expectation		
28.	Worries about social media		
29.	Getting performance feedback		
30.	Teammates' behaviours or attitude		
31.	Teammates' communication		
32.	Team/club atmosphere or culture		
33.	Goals of club/team		
34.	Facilities and equipment for training or competition		

35.	Nerves around selection		
36.	Weather conditions		
37.	Competition travel or accommodation		
38.	Competition rules and regulations		
39.	Distractions in training or competition		
40.	Safety when competing		
41.	Funding equipment, training or competition		
42.	Nutrition and hydration		
43.	Worries about getting schoolwork done		
44.	Missing out on time with family and friends		
45.	Having too much to do		
46.	Loneliness		
47.	Use of alcohol or drugs		
48.	Having to deal with discrimination or prejudice		
49.	Poor levels of sleep		
50.	Lack of energy		

How many ticks do you have in the first column? How many in the second? If you have lot more ticks in the first than in the second then you are likely to have lots of good coping mechanisms in place and be strongly protected by some of the psychological factors. If you have similar number of ticks in each column then you might want to spend some time working on some of the coping mechanisms in the rest of this chapter.

Five factors have been found to protect athletes from responding so negatively to many of the stressors which you come up against. The more of these you have the less stress you might feel in response to these stressors above taking place. One of these is out of our control (such as having a lots of positive personality traits) but others such as motivation (discussed above), confidence (covered in Chapter 4), being able to concentrate and focus (Chapter 6) and social support (Chapter 8) are all things we can work on and develop so we become better at buffering stress and managing our stress levels.

> Elite Insight: Joe Weatherly (cricket): I try to make sure everything outside of my cricket is aligned so when I go to training or matches I can just be me and everything is ok with my family, my house, my nutrition, my sleep. If things are messy at home or if things aren't just so I will really struggle to perform. I try to make sure that everything outside of my cricket is in a place which makes me happy and not stressed so that it helps me on the field.

We should also remember that even if we do have some stress in our sport for some of the time that it isn't always negative. We can learn a lot from what causes us stress (and focus on improving in those areas so we become a better athlete and feel happier) and we can get mentally stronger and more flexible from having dealt with the stress.

Just like the way we develop physical strength, by stressing our muscles and resting while they heal stronger, mentally too we need to do the same. We need some stressors to stretch us, and then when we rest and recover afterwards we realise we have become stronger. This helps us have a more helpful approach to stressors – that these struggles we have to go through will be valuable in making us a better athlete. In fact, some athletes purposely seek out difficult challenges, knowing they will cause some stress, because they know it helps them develop strength.

Activity: Where do I feel happiness and stress breathing exercise

A really nice way to track our stress and anxiety is to locate where you feel it in your body. This does sound really silly but try it. Take it seriously and you'll realise it is a really neat trick. You might feel happiness in your head and stress in your tummy. Or happiness in your chest and stress in your shoulders. First, we will look to find where you feel happiness.

- Close your eyes.
- Breathe in slowly through your nose. Feel that breath going right down inside you, as if it is going down to your belly button.
- Breathe out slowly through your mouth. Imagine the air you are breathing out is warm and comforting.
- Breathe like this three more times.
- Then, as you carry on breathing like this think about something really nice. Something that makes you happy. It could be your favourite food you have recently eaten, friends you have hung out with, a chat you had with your best mate or your favourite track. Focus on that memory and think deeply about it.
- Now, notice where in your body you feel that feeling. Scan your body all over and locate the feeling. Keep breathing. Keep thinking about the really nice, happy thing and identify where you feel it.
- Take one more deep breath in through the nose, out through the mouth and slowly open your eyes.

Question: I feel happiness in ...

Next, we will identity our stress zone.

- Close your eyes.
- Breathe in slowly through your nose. Feel that breath going right down inside you, as if it is going down to your belly button.
- Breathe out slowly through your mouth. Imagine the air you are breathing out is warm and comforting.
- Breathe like this three more times.
- Then, as you carry on breathing like this think about something that makes you feel really stressed or anxious. One of the

stressors you identified in the list above that makes you feel stressed. Focus on that issue and think deeply about it.

- Again, notice where in your body you feel that feeling. Scan your body all over and locate the feeling. Keep breathing. Keep thinking about that stressful thing and identify where you feel it.

- Take one more deep breath in through the nose, out through the mouth and slowly open your eyes.

Question: I feel stress in my ...

Once you have identified the place in your body where you feel anxiety then you can play with it. You can imagine the anxiety in that place in a more physical form. Give it a shape and a colour. What does it look like? Visualising it means you get to choose how to deal with it – do you want to drain it of its energy to help you attack your competition? Do you want to put it in a locked box while you do your competition? Having this distinction between you and the anxiety helps to distance it and to make it less impactful on your performance.

CONTROLLING STRESS BEFORE COMPETITIONS

Before competitions we may feel really stressed. Ideally, we would relax and then get into the best mindset for performance by focusing on the excitement of the challenge ahead. Unfortunately, it is often more likely that expectations and pressures will creep in and distract you so you start thinking about how you must win, or how you should play a certain way. The things going on around us (especially seeing other people practising, talking trash about how they plan to win or looking really fit) can add to that pressure so we need a technique to control the stress we feel ahead of competition. We can do this through simply not engaging and blocking them out through a pre-performance bubble. This helps you stay in control of what you see and hear and instead focus on the things which will improve your performance.

Activity: Pre-performance bubble

Your bubble can last as long as you want. Athletes in very big competitions will often go for about 24-48 hours, but if you are playing matches every week it is likely to be much shorter, maybe just a few hours. If you find yourself getting really stressed and wound up then maybe start it early – perhaps a day or two before your competition.

> Elite Insight: Dame Kelly Holmes (track): Two hours before the final I got to the warm up area, found a spot, lay down my towel and relaxed until it was time to warm up. I never really talk to anyone before a race but prefer to be in my own little world, focusing on the race to come.

Think about what you would do in your ideal competition build-up. What would you ideally do, and not have to do? Who would you hang out with and who would you avoid? The idea is to make your build-up super effective while protecting yourself from all the stresses and pressures that come up when you compete.

Areas to consider	Answer
How long before your event starts would you like your bubble to begin?	
• For a big important competition	
• For a regular tournament	
What sort of phone bubble would you like?	

• Phone off	
• Phone on with internet/social media off or using a non-smart phone	
• Phone on but messaging apps removed	
• Phone given to someone else so if there is an emergency they can let you know	
What sort of personal bubble would you like?	
• Hanging out with others	
• Hanging out on my own	
What sort of headphone bubble would you like?	
• Having music which gets me amped up	
• Having music which calms me down	
• No music – I like the quiet	
How will you fill time before competition?	
• Having movies to watch	
• Playing computer games	
• Warming up	
• Reading a book	
• Doing imagery	
• Chatting to coach, teammates or family	

A TUMMY FULL OF BUTTERFLIES

We can work on lots of strategies to remove some of the stressors and to deal better with them so we don't feel stress, but we don't actually want to completely lose our nerves ahead of competition. Nerves suggest we care about performing well and that is not only a good sign (indicating we have found the right sport) but also help us get our body and brain primed for action. We don't want too many nerves – then we have tipped into anxiety – but we do need some. How many will be personal to each of us. One way to think of it is that we need to feel the butterflies in our tummy, but as if they are gently flying in formation, not having a massive punch-up.

The punch-up feeling comes when our nerves have shot up and becomes anxiety. This is where you feel nervous, worried or apprehensive. When we feel these things, our brain switches into a threat mindset and, in order to prepare ourselves to flee the scary thing, our body is flooded with chemicals to help us fight (get aggressive), flight (run away) or freeze (hide). These chemicals increase our heart rate, breathing rate, blood pressure and amount of glucose in the blood, make us feel like we want to empty our stomach (either throwing up or rushing to the toilet) and give us muscle tension and fatigue which messes with our coordination. This is a rubbish position to be in as an athlete about to compete. It harms our performance and stops us from taking any enjoyment from competing. Studies have looked at athletes' emotions before events and tracked them against their performance. They found that those who were highly anxious performed worse. The more fine-muscle control you have in your sport (sports like shooting and snooker need lots) the bigger the negative impact of anxiety.

Question: How do I show my anxiety?

While the ideal level of nerves is different for each of us there are three things the amount of them tend to indicate:

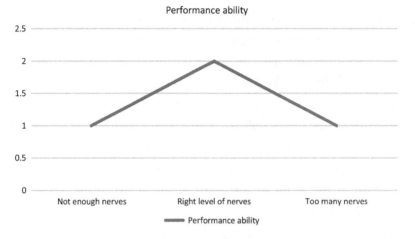

Performance ability

- Not enough nerves – we feel lethargic, we can't be bothered to prepare well, we are not fussed how the competition goes. We can call this an 'indifferent' mindset.

- The right amount of nerves – we are excited about performing. We call this 'challenge' mindset and look forward to what is ahead. It is often called your 'zone of optimal functioning'. If you have the right level of activation and feel like you have a challenge mindset then you might be more confident, be really proactive about achieving your goals, feel you have some control of the situations you find yourself in and feel pretty mentally tough.

- Too many nerves – we feel like the competition ahead is a threat and we are feeling anxious. This makes us feel dreadful and harms our chances of performing well. We call this a 'threat' mindset. If you constantly find yourself with a threat mindset you might have lower confidence, feel little control over your environment, try to avoid big opportunities and come up with reasons not to compete. You might catch yourself always thinking about what could go wrong (rather than what could go right).

Whether we are able to get to the right level of nerves is based on our personality traits, the mental skills we have developed and whether we feel we have the ability to deal with all the things which might stress us out. We talk about this as our activation level – what helps us feel ready and primed for best performance.

How do we get to our zone of optimal functioning where the butterflies dance and fly in formation but don't feel like they are having a big fight? Firstly, we need to become conscious of how we are feeling before each competition and reflect afterwards how it impacted our performance. Secondly, we need to go back to those stressors. When we have lots of stressors but also believe we have the resources (skills, time, teammates, coping mechanisms) to cope we are likely to go into this challenge state where we are excited about the competition and focus on what we need to do to be effective and to use great coping strategies. We can see the nerves as a signal that we love our sport and we care about doing it well.

If you look at the stressors, think about what you need in place to deal with them and decide you don't have what you need then you will find yourself in a threat state where you feel like you are in some type of danger and are going into battle. This harms our sporting performance because we feel anxious and question our abilities.

Activity: Translating stressors

Here is the same stressor but being felt by three different athletes on the same team. What type of mindset would you see each athlete having? Indifferent, threat or challenge?

Situation: Rugby match. Final game of the season. If the game is lost the team will be relegated down to the league below.

Tom: Tom is really excited for the match. He has been training loads recently and been watching videos of the competitors to learn their game plan and their weaknesses. Tom has been playing for years and this is not the first time he has played in a match with so much riding on it.

Tom has a _____ mindset.

Richard: Richard is looking forward to the match but mainly because he has heard the end of season parties are legendary. He has trained a bit but exams got in the way and they had to be his priority so while he doesn't feel fit enough to play he doesn't care that much.

Richard has a _____mindset.

Harry: Harry loves Rugby and wants to make it his career. He's applied to a premiership academy and a scout is coming today to watch him. This has made him super nervous. He's played this team before and lost and knows they can be quite rough to play against which worries him as he is coming back from an injury.

Harry has a _____ mindset.

DEVELOPING A CHALLENGE MINDSET

There is a prime level of activation for each of us which gets us to the right mental and physical place for competition. We can test where this sweet spot is through competition experience and post-competition analysis so we get the right balance of nerves and excitement. This challenge mindset makes our competitions much more comfortable to do. We can focus on all the things we need to do to perform brilliantly rather than worrying about all the things we could screw up. There are fortunately lots of ways through which we can develop this challenge mindset.

> Elite Insight: Diana Nyad (ultra swimming): We can't go back and wait for another day. This is it. So, am I going to continue complaining and cursing on just about every breath, or am I going to somehow summon a positive attitude and give this dream of mine all I've got? I don't utter one negative word the rest of the way.

MOVING FROM INDIFFERENCE TO CHALLENGE MINDSET

If we are too flat, feeling indifferent towards the competition ahead of us we can feel good that we don't have the nerves but we might also struggle to perform well without any pent-up energy there. When we have this indifference we need to amp ourselves up towards a challenge mindset. We need to boost our level of activation. How high you need to amp up to will depend on your own ideal activation level, your personality and what else is going on in your life.

Sometimes getting physical can help. Some athletes purposefully behave really energetically as if trying to wake themselves up. You might try a short jog, bounce up and down or tap your legs. While doing it you can breathe faster to psych yourself up. Short, deep breaths work well. A short phrase while you breath can also help: 'Energy in, tiredness out'. Or imagining something that is strong and powerful (a type of weather, a fictional hero, an animal full of strength) can ramp you up. Usain Bolt liked to joke and jump about beforehand to get his activation level up to where he needs it to be. The England Rugby player James Haskell has talked about how he used to slap himself in the face before matches to ramp up his activation.

Less painful than slapping yourself in the face is to use music. Music just before competition can get us into our zone of optimal functioning by increasing the amount of dopamine (a chemical involved in pleasure) in our brain which improves our mood and has been found to delay how long it takes us to feel fatigued.

Activity: Write a performance playlist

Research has found that music is a brilliant way to get us into our zone of optimal functioning. It can work well to help us ramp up into performance – to get the blood flowing, to get our excitement rising and to put us in a great headspace and find our challenge mindset.

The expert on music for sporting performance is Dr Costas Karageorghis. He is a professor in Sport & Exercise Psychology at Brunel University who has studied how to use music to get the best out of ourselves. He suggests if you are too calm and not psyched up enough you can raise your heart rate by listening to music with a rhythmic and syncopated (disrupted) rhythm. Most sports don't allow music when playing but we can listen to headphones before we start and when warming up to push our activation level up towards that feeling of challenge.

Here are the 10 rules for creating your performance playlist:

- Pick tracks that you know well and really like.
- Pick tracks that have some meaning to you.
- Try to find around 8 to 10 tracks to go on your playlist.
- Think about what you want from the music: to feel unstoppable, to smile, to feel more in control, to get focused, to boost energy?
- Have a couple of tracks on there which get you fired up and ready to go.
- Have a couple which use some inspirational words which feel like they talk to you.
- Use tracks with strong rhythms.

- Have a couple of tracks which bring back some positive memories or feelings.

- Listen to it on shuffle mode. We get a bigger buzz when we don't know what is coming.

- Try to find tracks that have extra associations, like coming from a movie where the hero overcomes adversity. This will raise your activation and helps you to feel unstoppable.

Elite Insight: Michael Johnson (sprinter): I put on my headphones, which I always used when I first arrived at the warm-up track to help me get into my own zone and focus, and to minimise distractions. Although I have always enjoyed a wide range of music from jazz to rap, 2Pac was one of my favourite artists. ... For the 200 I liked to get into a more forceful mode, so I had a playlist of rap music to match the more aggressive approach needed for the 200 metres. For this race I chose 2Pac's 'Me against the world'. ... The tempo was slower than I wanted but it was saying all the right things.

MOVING FROM THREAT INTO CHALLENGE MINDSET

Tougher than moving up from indifference to challenge is dialling things down from threat to challenge. It doesn't feel great when our body is tight, our oxygen entry is restricted and we feel under pressure.

To replicate a pressure posture raise your shoulders towards your ears. What does this do to your posture? It will put you into a position where your breathing moves towards your upper chest. This makes it more rapid and shallow. This is similar to how you will feel when anxious.

To move towards how you would want to feel when you perform, lower your shoulders, lift your head, send your chest slightly forward, breathe deep – as if you are trying to send that air you take in down to your belly button. This is how you should be feeling before competition. Calm, coping and ready to take on whatever comes.

So how do we get this 'calm, coping' feeling? We do it by breaking the cycle of anxiety to 'deactivate' ourselves a little. We have two routes to try for this. Firstly, changing things physically and secondly, learning to interpret and respond to those thoughts differently. Let's focus on the physical side first. There are lots of things to try here.

> Elite Insight: Michael Phelps (swimming): Mom and I used to go through relaxation and programming techniques at home. … I would tighten my right hand into a fist and relax it, then do the same with my left hand as a way of learning to deal with tension. At night, before falling asleep, I would lie on my bed and she would read to me from the book and I would practice.

When preparing for a competition everything our body does feeds into our brain – as it is a signal – telling it how we are feeling. Short, sharp breaths tell our brain we are panicking, and in difficulty. If we focus on breathing slowly to keep everything else working well we can control our brain better. This means that to physically calm down the responses in our body we need to change our breathing patterns. We usually breathe about 12–18 breathes per minute. In stressful situations that rises. Our aim, if we want to feel calmer, is to get it down to around 5–8 breaths per minute.

Activity: Colourful breathing

Colourful breathing is a great technique to calm ourselves down as it is short and easy to do but also really effective. It means you get oxygen deeper into your lungs and refreshes your posture. We can use it in sport but also any time we feel under stress – exams, big social event, dealing with an argument. To do it effectively we need about one minute.

- First pick off two colours. They could be your favourite two colours, your club kit colours or your favourite sports team. Here, just as an example, we'll use blue and red.
- Think about your lungs finishing just behind your belly button. You'll want to see it going in and out as you do the activity.
- Breathe in through your nose as you count to four. Imagine that air that is going into your nose is hot red air.
- Hold the air behind your belly button for a count of two.
- Breathe out cool blue air through your month as you count to six.
- Repeat four or five times. Until you feel calmer.

Other ways to calm down our activation ...

Music

Music is great for ramping up, but it is also really handy if you find yourself with a threat mindset and need to dial everything down. Professor Karageorghis says that music can be very effective at making us more chilled, so he suggests if you are very nervous before a race listen to slow, warming music to keep a lid on anxiety. He tells us that Dame Kelly Holmes (double Olympic champion) used to listen to Alicia Keys before races to calm herself down.

Coping methods

We know that when we have a threat mindset we are most likely to try to cope with the stress of the situation by ranting at friends or family or by hiding away from a situation – people might even not enter events or competitions they would deep down love to do because of this fear. A much better type of coping mechanism to go for is known as 'solution-focused coping' where we actively break down the problem into smaller parts and work out how to fix them. Perhaps you get into a threat mindset every time you compete against a specific team and would try to find a reason not to be selected when the team sheet gets put up. Solution-focused coping would see you work out that you dislike a couple of their players who are overly aggressive, that every time they step out of line you'll ask the referee to intervene, that everytime they start shouting at you you'll imagine them as Minnie Mouse and then you'll do some imagery to practise coping well with their behaviour.

Boosting confidence

If your head is full of confidence it blocks out a lot of the anxieties. If you know you can do well and use the skills you have learnt you are less likely to feel under threat. Boosting your confidence is then a great tactic to use to help your challenge mindset develop. Lots of the ideas in Chapter 4 will help you become more confident.

Targets over trophies

One of the reasons we get into the threat mindset is because we are thinking about the outcomes of the event ahead of us. Will we win, lose, make a prat of ourselves? These thoughts just pile on a load of pressure and anxiety and increase our risk of mentally checking out mid competition if the score starts to head in the wrong direction. In short, we are focusing on the trophy (that is a possible outcome) rather than on the target (which might help us do well enough to win the trophy).

Elite Insight: Diana Nyad (ultra swimming): If you're doing 17 hours, you don't let your mind wander to imagine how hour 15 is going to be when you are still on hour one or two or three. You need to use conscious discipline to keep yourself from projecting forward.

Focusing on the targets means we can concentrate on all the tasks that help us get ready to compete. It means we work out what will create a great outcome (the how to do it), rather than on the outcome itself. To stay focused on the targets we need to pick process goals before competition that we want to achieve. They could be things like these: I will stay patient, I will mark my rival continually, I will count to two before shooting or I will practise helpful thinking. This will give you positive tasks to focus on so you can be far calmer and more successful.

Being really well prepared

If we haven't done the training or don't know the venue or the type of competitors we are up against we are very likely to feel under threat on competition day. Anyone would – it is a difficult position to put ourselves in. Preparing really well is a good way to stay in the challenge mindset zone. We can do this in the build-up to a competition by training really hard and putting lots of effort and focus in. It really helps us feel more in control. On the day it can be a different matter though.

Some athletes try to grasp this feeling of control by following a super-stition. You might have one yourself. Lots of people have them – includ-ing some of the world's best athletes:

- Serena Williams (tennis) is reported to tie her shoelaces a specific way, bounce the ball five times before her first serve and twice before her second and wear the same pair of socks during a winning streak.

- Ronaldo (football) was said to always step onto the pitch with his right foot first.

- Michael Jordan (basketball) always wore a pair of North Carolina practice shorts underneath his Chicago Bulls ones.

- Laura Kenny (cycling) once won a junior race wearing a wet sock and has ever since stepped on a wet towel before races.

- Björn Borg (tennis) prepared for Wimbledon by growing a beard and wearing the same Fila shirt.

- Rafael Nadal (tennis) crosses lines with his right foot, arrives with one tennis racket in his hand, eats his energy gels in a specific way and lines up his water bottles in an orderly line, with all the labels pointing in the same direction.

- Sprinter Jodie Williams (athletics) had a lucky elephant charm that she claims took her through 151 races unbeaten. When she lost the elephant, she lost her next race. She then had an elephant tattooed on her ankle instead.

- Tiger Woods (golf) always wears red on the final day of a tournament.

The superstitions usually arise after a great performance which the athlete wants to recreate. They seem completely illogical, and theoretically they are. Wearing a red T-shirt or having a soggy sock will not physically improve your focus or technique – but if they make you believe you will be more in control and have created the right conditions for high performance then they can be of benefit. Some superstitions can be helpful if they help you actually get ready to perform – a specific warm-up, hitting your legs to trigger their readiness, taking an energy gel and a swing of water as they give a physical benefit and distract you from your anxiety or nerves. When you do your superstition before you start competing the behaviour triggers adrenalin which helps you feel ready to get going and makes you feel 'I'm good to go'. However, there is a downside. A big one. If the superstition involves a charm, or a specific piece of kit, and that goes missing then all control feels lost and you will feel unable to perform well. You will have lost before you have even started.

To gain the same level of control but in a more effective and safer manner, you can work on routines instead. These give you a much better chance of success because they involve meticulous planning. They mean you arrive in plenty of time, have all the kit you need, have eaten and drunk enough, do a great warm-up and practise any key mental skills. They keep you focused on the now (and not on future potential outcomes), and this gives you a much stronger control of the controllables than a superstition might. They give true security that you have done all you can. And get you warmed up and ready to perform both physically and mentally. You can create your own personal pre-performance routine to achieve this.

Activity: Pre-performance routine

Your pre-performance routine should be designed to fit your sport and your lifestyle. In some sports you might have to register, pay entry and get equipment checked the day before, others you rock up to the venue 30 minutes before the starting whistle. You can adapt your routine to match these requirements.

> Elite Insight: Rebecca Adlington (swimming): Before races I focused on preparation. … I did have a set routine. I had to be out of the warmup pool an hour before. Making sure I had time to have a snack, refuel, get changed into my racing suit. For me mentally, it was just about trying to stay really calm and really relaxed and not trying to exert myself in any way emotionally just as much as physically.

Start by picking an event you are working towards and find out what time you will start your competition. Work your way backwards around this 12-hour clock to put in all the activities and tasks you will need to do before you start. The areas to cover are listed below along with lots of questions to ask yourself:

Training: Do I want to train or exercise the day of or the day before the event, and, if so, what shall I do?

Support: Who do I like to be there watching and supporting me? What do I like them to say to me beforehand?

Kit and equipment: When will I pack my kit bag? Have I a kit and equipment list I use? When did I last check my equipment was working well? Where can I store my equipment during the event? Do I have spares of everything important?

Travel: How will I travel to my competition? Am I going with my parents or other team members? What time do I need to leave my house? Do I have the address of the venue? Have we checked if there is parking? Will I need to pay for it?

Food: Do I have a pre-race dinner that I like to eat the night before? What works for me for breakfast on competition day? Do I have it in the house? If I'm staying away will I be able to get my usual breakfast foods? What time should I eat breakfast? Do I want any nutrition before I start?

Warm-up: How much warm-up do I need to do to feel good? Will I avoid people or chat to my friends? Do I want my headphones on while I warm up? What is my best warm-up music?

Mental skills: Will I use any mental skills before we start? What will I use to get into the challenge mindset: imagery, my performance playlist, colourful breathing or working through my coping mechanisms for the scary stuff?

Here is an example routine for a Fencer whose competition begins at 11am.

The more you practise your pre-performance routine the more beneficial it becomes, so it is good to do before every event so that when you get to the big ones you really care about (and are likely to be more anxious over) it really has a positive impact.

Elite Insight: Mo Farah (running): Every athlete has a pre-race routine they like to stick to. I like to shave my head – to feel my scalp smooth, the refreshing sense of slapping cold water over it. It's a sort of ritual, I guess. Then I'll listen to some tunes. Depending on my mood it'll be some Tupac or maybe Dizzee Rascal. All morning long I'll be drinking water to keep myself hydrated. 3 hours before the start of the 10,000 metres race, I'll head down to the stadium and make my way to the warm-up area.

These activities and strategies are all great to change our behaviours so our brain doesn't react to threat so dramatically. We can build them into habits so they become part of who we are as an athlete.

An entirely different route to go down through to reduce our feelings of threat so we are better able to nurture a challenge mindset can also be really effective and that is a more mindful approach.

I suspect right now you are rolling your eyes. 'Mindfulness' has been a buzz word for years and, while very helpful for some, it can feel very alien to athletes who spend so much of their time running around and being active. Who wants to sit still and meditate when you could be out doing more interesting stuff? I get you. Athletes often struggle with this approach but those who adopt and incorporate it within their sport find huge benefits.

What mindfulness is really good for is making us really self-aware of what we think. When we become really aware we can be more active about what we do with those thoughts. When we get really good at noticing the thoughts, we can start to distance ourselves from them. You may have heard the phrase 'You are not your thoughts' and mindfulness helps us remember and value this.

Elite Insight: Rafael Nadal (tennis): Enduring means accepting things as they are and not as you would wish them to be and then looking ahead, not behind, which means taking stock of where you are and thinking coolly.

It means instead of trying to block out the feelings we might struggle with (especially the ones which make us feel under threat) we can accept that some of these worries are ok so we can accept the thoughts exist (rather than trying to ignore or squash them) but be much cleverer about what we do with them.

For athletes specifically, studies have found using this approach can help improve performance and enhance your activation skills so you get better at being aware of what your body is trying to tell you, helps you be smarter at sifting through information so you can make better tactical decisions and lets you have more control over your behaviour.

When the USA BMX team learnt how to use it they improved their self-awareness, noticed more of their body sensations and felt more present in competition, and when their brains were scanned it was seen that they even responded differently to physical stress. On competition day their coach noticed a physical response too; they were able to get out of the gates faster.

Activity: Mindfulness

The key point to focus on is that you might notice your thoughts but you do not judge them. You are an observer of your thoughts. You are consciously paying attention to what you think so you really notice it – but not to engage with those thoughts. No beating yourself up!

To begin you need somewhere quiet. It is best not to lie down in case you fall asleep (athletes' bodies are often keen to nap!) but instead have a comfy chair where you can put your hands to the side or resting on top of your legs. You need to close your eyes, take a really deep breath so you can feel your lungs filling behind your belly button, drop your shoulders, and relax your hands. Feel your belly button and chest rise and fall and you slowly breathe in and out. As you take each breath notice the cool air you take in, and how warm it is as you breathe it out. Don't try to control your breath too much. Let it flow.

As you get into a natural rhythm start to move your thoughts away from your breathing and instead notice what you are thinking. Don't judge those thoughts. Just notice they exist. If you find yourself getting dragged into thinking about anything deeply move your focus back to your breathing.

Keep going for 10 minutes. To see how you get on. Jot down afterwards how it felt, anything specific you noticed or thoughts that snuck into your head regularly.

Day 1	
Day 2	
Day 3	
Day 4	
Day 5	
Day 6	
Day 7	

If you find this is ok and you are able to manage the ten minutes you can use this mindfulness practice to develop your 'thought labelling'. It helps you get better emotional control by putting your worrisome thoughts into words. When people using this technique have been studied in MRI machines it was found that thought labelling reduces the amount of emotion they felt when they noticed those thoughts, so they are less likely to feel under threat and the thoughts don't have such a negative effect. Labelling our thoughts also helps us feel more comfortable discussing them so we are better able to do something positive; such as using solution-focused coping methods (rather than hiding away or ranting to anyone who will listen).

Activity: Thought labelling

As you finish your mindfulness session ask yourself which thoughts you noticed. Scribble them down. Are there any themes? Does something similar come up over and over? These will be the ones to label. It is entirely up to you as to how you label them, as they will be so personal to your own situation. Some might be quite general – 'scared about competing', 'worried about rejection' or 'missing my friends' – but others maybe really specific – 'lonely at training camp', 'excited about trying my new equipment' or 'frustrated I'm not improving'. Once you have a number of these you'll start to get an idea which ones are most on your mind; class them into helpful or unhelpful and make a decision on whether it is something you want to deal with it or not.

You might want to pick on some and be proactive about resolving them. On others it might not be solvable, it might not even be true, in fact they often aren't true, they are just our perception so instead we get used to distancing ourselves from them. We do this by stating 'the thought is not a fact, it is just a thought'. It moves us from:

I am a rubbish athlete → I think I am a rubbish athlete.

We can add a step into this to distance ourselves even further:

I think I am a rubbish athlete → I am noticing that I think I am a
   rubbish athlete.

This distancing makes it clearer it is just a thought and not reality.

Social media pressures

One of the biggest causes of anxiety and stress in sport are comparisons. They are everywhere in sport, and technology and social media do not help at all. Comparisons become a huge pressure. It may be constant team chat on WhatsApp groups, worrying about your results being gossiped about or made fun of, videos of you performing being shared or seeing what everyone else is doing on feeds or apps and feeling left behind. The comparisons, the gossip, the FOMO, can all play havoc with your mind – especially ahead of competitions. Everything is in your face. You might go for a run or a bike ride and love it but if you get home and upload it onto a tracking website like Strava you might see a teammate or rival has gone faster, or longer and suddenly feel like a failure.

In sport these can be really damaging because we have something called a 'halo effect' which comes when we let the impression we have of other athletes from just one area of their life (like a photo of them on Instagram looking fit and happy) influence how we feel about them in other areas. It means we end up making assumptions about other elements of their life (like they look fit and happy so must be at the top of their game) just because we know one positive thing about them and we end up building them out of all proportion. There is also an 'availability bias' where we use the information we have recently heard about them when making decisions or opinions. So, we might have seen lots and lots of pictures of them training so assume they are fighting fit. You won't have seen the tears when they can't perform or the frustration that whatever they do they are not getting any better. They may not even be training much at all but the app's algorithm is just showing their pictures more often than others. We then believe they are unstoppable and that can self-sabotage our own confidence.

SUCCESS STORY: CHARLIE HODGSON

Charlie Hodgson played rugby for Sale Sharks, Saracens and England over a 17-year professional career. He played for England 38 times and won the Guinness Premiership at Sale Sharks and multiple domestic and European premiership titles with Saracens. He is the leading premiership points scorer of all time.

Growing up I didn't find sport a pressure. I always used sport as just something I loved doing. And I still do. When I was growing up my goal wasn't to become a professional Rugby player – it would have been nice but I didn't really know much about the professional game and I didn't have a massive amount of role models in Rugby Union to look at. I had the successes of being picked for Yorkshire and the North of England schoolboys but I wasn't overly concerned if that was going to lead to a professional contract. I just loved playing the game so I wouldn't say I had an expectation of what came. I didn't have a clue what I wanted to do and maybe that was a good thing.

Sometimes I look back at my career and think if I had not goal kicked I probably would have enjoyed the experience much more. In matches, if I knew I wasn't goal kicking, it would almost take a bit of pressure off me in my approach to the games. I knew if I missed a goal then I would be letting other people down so for me that was the added pressure, an added expectation I had of myself internally and externally from players and coaches and the crowd.

I never really looked too far ahead in advance and if I am honest I don't think I even did that as a professional. You are very lucky in Rugby in a sense that you have got a game every single week so you have got a very short time frame to do something, to feed back and then you go again. And that is the bit I really enjoyed about it and I think that helps you stay in the moment of enjoying that process and being there.

Being prepared helps how you feel. It is the winging it which gives you the anxiety. The more prepared you are the more in control you feel and of course that helps reduce those feelings of anxiety.

Before a match was the bit I hated most. It is the one thing I don't miss, that whole build up, that three hour build up from meeting to eating to just sitting around waiting. You can't remove those nerves – they are a good thing – you need them. I was able to see that the nerves were helpful to getting prepared to play. The time when you don't have them is a time when you start to worry. For me they never disappeared.

The one way that I used to deal with it was being in control. I think when you are sitting there in a meeting room and you are waiting I think that is when those nerves tend to get the better of you. For me it was just about getting outside and doing something that was going to be proactive. To keep me in control of what was to come and what was going to happen.

My pre-match routine developed organically. It never changed. We would eat the same meal of chicken and pasta and tomato sauce. Then I would go outside to do my kicking practice. The experience being outside and running around and kicking and practising means you are in the moment so it takes your mind away from what is to come. I felt when I had done that then I had ticked off all the boxes to say I had done everything I can and if it goes wrong it goes wrong. That element of routine for me was the way I could remove those nerves and the feelings of anxiety before games.

I remember Jason Robinson once being asked about superstitions and he said 'I don't believe in them because you give yourself a reason if things don't go well.' That really resonated with me so from then on I decided to just control what I can control.

I think one of the hardest bits was perhaps the couple of minutes before you go out to play. I would be lying if I said I didn't have those times when I thought "what am I doing here" or "I can't do this" or "I am really out of my depth" but you have got no choice. There are certainly moments when you feel quite scared about the situation you are going into. But at the same time there is no going back and once the whistle goes and you are into it you are in the moment again and you are happy doing what you do best.

CHAPTER **3**

I can improve

How do we get better? We get faster, higher, further or more skilled by working on two things: being braver and pushing harder. The attitude needed to be both brave and to use persistent effort can be learnt but it takes discipline, rehearsal and effort to ingrain it inside your head. Once installed and practised it will take you far – in all areas of your life. In this chapter we will look at exactly how to do this.

BRAVERY

Sport can be whatever we want it to be – fun, a great social life, a way to cope with difficult things and can be fantastic for our physical and mental health. For each of those things we need to approach it with a suitable mindset. If we want to be brilliant at it then we need the right mindset, one which helps us stretch ourselves to be brave.

To be brave we need to leave our comfort zone. Comfort zones keep us safe – stopping us from putting ourselves in scary situations. But they also hold us back. They place limits on us and if we stay in ours we will never know how good we could be. If we want to be brilliant at our sport, we need to stretch ourselves to try harder and do tougher things. We also need to risk failing. If we are continually worrying about what might happen if we miss a goal or lose a competition then we can never reach new heights. In fact, studies show that when we focus on doing well we tend to be more successful than when we focus on not doing badly, perhaps because we don't behave so cautiously and hold ourselves back. Mentally this approach can feel harder, particularly if you have spent a long time with the more negative mindset. We either worry we will be judged by others if we show how much we are trying to achieve something or we will put in lots of time and effort and energy and invest so much in our sport that we miss out on other things and still risk it not paying off.

It is easier to be brave when we have the right support behind us, when we know it is absolutely fine to take a risk and that trying new things will be celebrated rather than punished. It means we need to feel safe and trusted with our coaches, teammates and parents.

Question: What stops you from leaving your comfort zone?

Question: What would make you leave your comfort zone?

CONTROL

This approach on doing well in competition, rather than focusing on not messing up, means we should be concentrating on the things we can control, not worrying about all the things we can't.

> Elite Insight: Jason Kenny (cycling): I try not to worry, because worrying has always seemed pointless to me. Can you change something? Then change it. If you can't let it go.

One way to do this is to be really clear on what we can control so we can positively influence these elements and stop wasting energy on all the things that we cannot influence. A control scale is a way to identify where our efforts should be going.

> Elite Insight: Emma Wiggs (paracanoeing): So much of the outcome is uncontrollable. What is controllable is our delivery and execution of it.

Activity: Control scale

There are hundreds of different elements which impact our performance. What do you have control of, just some influence of and no control of at all? This is a really good activity to do in the week before a competition. It can help you develop some task-focused actions which will make a really positive impact on your performance. On the next page are 21 to think about and drop into the 3 sections below:

I have complete control over these things	I have some influence	I have no control at all over these things

Your attitude	Your own worries (the things which tend to stress you out more than others)	Your warm-up
Your effort levels	The course/pitch you are competing on	How supporters (both yours and competitors) behave
Your behaviours	The venue	The behaviour and decisions (of officials or referees)
Your competitors	Weather	The date and time of the event
How your competitors behave	Equipment	The result
The mental skills you use	Nutrition and hydration available	Your performance routines and plans.
Your body language	Logistics (like travel, costs or organisation)	Who comes to watch you

If we want to gently stretch our comfort zone without too much fear we can gradually try different things. They will still be in our sport and beneficial to our long-term performance goals but ways to try something a bit different. You could pick things around your fitness, specific sporting skills, maybe a different event in your sport, a different attitude to competition, working on flexibility or strength or different types of competition goals. For example, a rugby player could try:

- A different event in the same sport – playing sevens for a session.
- A different type of recovery – wearing compression gear or trying a yoga class.
- A different sport – swimming as cross training, cycling to turn legs over without being weightbearing or ballet to improve core strength.

Another way to stretch our comfort zone in a way that feels safe is to prepare incredibly well. When we know there are some solid foundations in place it is easier to be brave and go above and beyond our usual levels of effort or approach.

We can be braver when we have planned for all the things which could go wrong. If we have thought about the things we fear, consider how to prevent them and set up a plan in case they still happen we won't be quite so weighed down by fear.

To do this we need to really identify what is holding us back – what makes us fearful of going 'all in' to our competitions. The honesty required for this is tough but once you have a list written down of all the things that weigh you down with fear you can work on a plan. This stops us from burying our head in the sand and means instead we actively deal with those worries. We call it 'what if' planning.

Activity: What-if planning

There are three steps to this. The first step is to think about your next big competition and write down every single worry you have about it. Both big and small worries should be on there. Even if they seem irrational or silly it is important to put them down. We have given you space for 10 worries here though you may have up to 30 or 40 if it is a really big event that you have been training for a long time.

Worries you might have could include:

Injury	Losing motivation
Unfairness in judging/refereeing	Shoelace coming undone and tripping over
Seeing negative comments on social media	Getting disqualified
Getting distracted	Losing against someone who is lower ranked
Losing temper if you start doing badly	Equipment failure
Feeling ill	Toilet issues
Getting hurt mid event	

Worry	To prevent it happening I will ...	If ... then I will ...

Look through each issue you have put down and consider a couple of ways you could prevent it from happening. This means you can put in place those actions and make it much less likely to happen.

Then work on the 'if ... then' plan for what you would do if it did happen. This means if the worst happens you don't have to think what you do – you already have a plan so you will be much less flustered and just get on with it.

We can take the swimmer Michael Phelps as a brilliant example here. Maybe a worry he had before his races was his goggles leaking. In his book *No Limits* he tells the story of exactly how he dealt with this. He talks of how his coach Bob would arrange practices and drills around the idea of being uncomfortable to see how he responded under pressure. The idea was if he could deal with whatever it was when he was tired, he could deal with anything that came his way. Once his coach even stepped on his goggles to see how he reacted. This became incredibly helpful in the 200 IM (Individual Medley) in the Olympic Final when his goggles leaked. He could see a little until 100m to go and they got more and more blurry. With 75 metres to go they were completely full and he couldn't see a thing. He carried on, focused on just counting the strokes and not only won the race but set a new World Record in the process.

CREATE SOME MAGIC POWERS: SUPERHERO OR ALTER EGO

When we think about being brave we might imagine that we could be a lot braver if we had some superpowers. Well, why can't we? Our powers are unlikely to be climbing the walls like Spiderman or changing the weather like Storm in X-Men but they can be something we really focus on developing into a super strength that will help us really stand out and give us a massive shot of confidence that gives us an edge and makes us less intimidated by our competitors.

> Elite Insight: Jonny Brownlee (triathlon): My personality totally changes in a race. I can go from being perfectly pleasant to brutally aggressive, shouting at anyone. The Jekyll and Hyde nature of it doesn't bother me; it's part of the race and I'll do anything not to lose.

Your super strength will be fairly unique to you in the group you train with. It might be that you have a really strong start if you are a netballer, that you have a great sprint finish as a track runner or that you rarely foul as a long jumper. In any sport it could be that you are always able to bounce back from setbacks or that you can block out pressure in big competitions and go in excited. Having this element, this superpower tucked away in your back pocket doesn't mean you stop training on your weaknesses or ignore other things but it does mean you feel stronger and less intimidated by your competitors.

Question: What is your sporting superpower?

Question: What could you do to pump up your superpower?

If you can't find a sporting superpower (and that is absolutely fine – it can take many years to develop one) then we need to develop one and incorporate it into our sporting identity instead; we call this an 'alter ego'. Tiger Woods did this. Or rather his father did. He was named Eldrick Woods when born but his dad called him Tiger when he was three as he wanted him to behave on the golf course in a more assertive way. Dwayne Johnson, previously an American footballer, named himself 'The Rock' when he moved into wrestling as he needed to distance himself from his shy and humble character and instead wanted to pretend to be full of ego and empty of remorse. Alter egos can be particularly helpful in sports where aggression is needed, as it can be hard to develop that aggression if you are naturally a calmer, gentler person.

> Elite Insight: Ronda Rousey (MMA): When I walk out of the hotel room, I feel like superman stepping out of the phone booth – chest out, cape billowing behind him. Unstoppable, Unbeatable. Only instead of an S, I have the UFC logo emblazoned across my chest. My mean face is on. From the minute I leave the room I'm in fight mode.

So, if you are in a sport where you are really having to mentally step outside your comfort zone in order to have the right characteristics to be successful then an alter ego can be really useful and make you feel much more comfortable competing.

Activity: Becoming your own sporting superhero

Flip back to Chapter 1 and read your performance profile. What areas are you missing? What characteristics would help you to have that which you haven't yet mastered?

You are not trying to create a whole new character. We keep your physical skills, tactics and techniques. We keep your hopes and dreams. What we add in is the approach or attitude or mindset that your character has. Your alter ego is still you – but with a few additional helpful characteristics mixed in.

To bring your character to life think about:

- The name of your character:

- The music your character will listen to:

- The mental skills your character would use:

- The statement your character will make to motivate themself:

- What type of kit your character would wear (if they have choice over it):

- The super strength of your character:

- The approach your character takes to competition:

If you practise getting into your alter ego it will help you feel more comfortable and efficient in switching it on and off so when it comes to competition day you can put your character's music in your ears, state their mantra and get into your performance mode.

OUR OWN BIGGEST RIVAL

When we set ourselves a big goal – one which matters to us and needs us to be brave – we are taking a big risk. What if we mess up? We can't shrug it off and pretend it doesn't matter to us because it does, so we open ourselves up to failing. Failing is scary. A way many of us protect ourselves is by self-sabotaging. We make lots of small failings – turning up late for training, not checking out courses or venues, eating or drinking things we know are not healthy or setting goals which are too easy, all of which minimize our chances at performing at our best. What these small, excusable fails do is give us what feels like a valid excuse for when we fail at the big goal. It means while we might fail at a few small things we are protected from total failure because we have a reason for that failure. We then feel more protected from other people's judgement. The problem is we are making everything harder for ourselves and less likely to be successful.

The most common form of self-sabotage is procrastination. How often do you have a long list of things to be getting on with and find yourself wasting time? Every time we procrastinate, we have less time left to do the things we need. And whatever we do while we are procrastinating is usually not that enjoyable as we spend that time in stressful anticipation of what we still need to do.

Question: Which part of my sport do I tend to procrastinate over?

Activity: Spot and stop your sabotaging behaviours

Look down each of the columns and circle what feels relevant to you.

Get aware. What do you do that negatively impacts your sport performance?	Triggers. What tends to trigger your self-sabotaging behaviour?	Reasons. Why do you self-sabotage?
Procrastination over training	After an argument	So I don't risk properly failing
Not preparing properly for competition	Feeling negative	I am afraid I will reach my limits
Not drinking enough water	Hungry or thirsty	Working hard hurts
Not sleeping or resting enough	Tiredness	I don't want other people to judge me
Eating non-nutritious food	Following a bad day or training session	I don't feel confident enough to achieve my goals
Messing about in training sessions	Fear of failure	I want to control my failure rather than it controlling me
Taking it easy in a training session	A practice session which is really difficult	I don't feel I deserve success
Going out making myself too tired to train properly	Low confidence	I feel like a fraud in my sport
Not doing physio, rehab or strength and conditioning exercises	Boredom	I'm not the kind of person who is successful
Not following the training plan properly	Feeling inadequate compared to others	I like the feeling of drama

Now that you have circled your self-sabotaging habits and identified what triggers them and why you use them, you can make a plan. Look back to Chapter 1 when you made your goal. You can use it to make your self-sabotage plan:

- My goal is …

- My self-sabotage is stopping me reaching my goal by …

- Next time I find myself starting to self-sabotage I will …

PUSHING HARDER

Humans, thousands of years ago, came from an environment of scarcity. It was hard and dangerous to find food and shelter so our brains were shaped to preserve energy and waste as little effort as possible. This makes us naturally lazy and continually looking for an easy option. Obviously, this is not helpful in sport. To be a great athlete we need to find an override button. Some of us, like Charlie Hodgson, have this naturally. Many of us do not.

> Elite Insight: Charlie Hodgson (rugby): I had an internal driver to win. I think I have always been very competitive from a very early age. When I wasn't playing rugby I would try and hang around in the local fields in the hope I would get invited to play football with some boys who were older than me. … I would always want to test myself against these guys who were two or three years older than me. I loved that experience and I loved pushing myself in that experience so that internal driver to compete was always there.

Many years ago scientists thought of our bodies as machines where our ability to work harder was limited by our muscles running out of energy and getting too tired to carry on. We now know that even when our muscles are really tired there is actually still some energy there so it is something else that is holding us back. The latest thinking is that what stops us is firstly not having a goal that motivates us enough and then, when we are motivated, still feeling like the effort required to achieve that goal is too hard. When we boost our motivation and make the efforts feel easier, we become much better at pushing ourselves in sport.

MOTIVATION

First up, to be able to work harder, we need to max out our motivation. We can think about motivation as the energy in our brain which determines how we behave and directs the ways we think and feel when we work on our target. We need that brain energy to be in place before we can use any other skills or strategies. It will impact everything in your sport: your physical conditioning, your technical and tactical training, mental preparation and general lifestyle including sleep, diet, school and friendships. The good news is, if you pick the right goal, you have complete control over your motivation. And when you are fully motivated you will put in lots of time and effort into practice and competition.

Our motivation is usually pretty strong when we start in our sport. We progress really quickly, we are learning lots of impressive skills we couldn't do before and everything feels new and exciting. We see ourselves getting better and better and we are making new friends and feeling fit and strong. And we might have coaches wanting us to focus on competing in competitions rather than just completing practice sessions. Everything then becomes outcome focused and so the sport takes on more importance and our original motivation (to have fun, to meet new friends, to get fit) falls away.

There are three types of motivation: amotivation, extrinsic and intrinsic. Read through the descriptions here and think about where you get your motivation from.

> Amotivation: We have low energy, can't be bothered to train. Find ourselves regularly complaining. We don't do well in competition and we don't really care. We might cut-short training or skip it entirely. We are not committed, our effort levels are low and our passion for our sport has dried up. After a while we may quit our sport.

> Extrinsic: We compete for the success it brings us. We love congratulations from others. We enjoy winning trophies. We look for our name in the results section in the paper or on websites.

We have friends in our sport we like to see and we enjoy the improvement. This type of motivation is helpful if you are goal driven as we have tangible goals to work towards and will get that buzz of success when we reach them.

Intrinsic: We have a pure joy from doing in our sport. We love feeling like we have improved and rarely have to persuade ourselves to go to training. We don't always need to do well – we just enjoy the physical feeling of doing it. This is a great motivation to have as we know we will enjoy any competitions or training sessions even if the outcome is not great.

If you feel like you are struggling with your motivation and that perhaps you related best to the amotivation or the extrinsic motivation, then we can move closer to intrinsic motivation by putting the five pillars of motivation in place:

1. A great goal. You need to have a goal which genuinely excites you and makes you want to get out practising. Without that it is easy to get distracted. Check back to Chapter 1 to make sure your goal does this.
2. Skills. We all want to feel competent – to feel like we have the ability required and have mastered the skills needed to achieve our goal.
3. Community. It is vital we have a sense of belonging and know we sit within our sporting or club community where we are accepted and encouraged.
4. Ownership. You need to own your goals. If your coach or parents have told you what you should be working towards and you don't agree then it is going to be super hard to drum up the effort required. We need to be in control of our choices to put the required effort levels in.
5. Fun. We need to enjoy what we do.

If we are missing any of these elements then we can focus on developing that element and our motivation should rise. When we have all five elements in place our motivation should be high, we should feel intrinsic and we will be driven to achieve our goals.

But, motivation is not limitless. I could offer you £1 million to set a new personal best or win your next match and I can imagine you would put a huge amount of preparation and effort into doing do. Offering you an additional £1 million would obviously be nice but it probably wouldn't make that much difference to your motivation. At the point we max out our motivation we need to make our efforts feel easier.

MAKING IT FEEL EASIER

Having a high perception of effort – where everything you are doing in a competition feels hard – can become a barrier to performance as we feel worse and are more likely to pull out of our event. There are lots of techniques that we use every day when practising or training that help us feel like our efforts have become easier – training harder (so our bodies get more used to the effort levels), learning better physical techniques (so we do our sport more efficiently) and taking in nutrition which gives us energy and hydration. There are also lots of competition strategies we can use to lower our perception of effort when we most care about our performance. We can consider each, one by one.

Chunk up your competition

Chunking is an approach we use to break down a competition into much smaller pieces so it feels less intimidating and pressured. It can help you break everything into bite sized things that are easier to face. As we get through each section we give ourselves a reminder that we can cope and get through the periods we thought were hard which boosts our confidence and helps us feel like everything is more manageable.

When we use chunking we can give ourselves a goal for each section of our competition so we can be more focused in our strategies – this is a great performance enhancer. An additional boost to this is that this 'tick box' of sectional goals achieved in our head releases a brain chemical called dopamine which gives us a surge of pleasure so we feel really positive too.

Mentally taper

When we have a lot going on in our lives we can get mentally fatigued. This is especially likely as junior athletes when you have to fit in school, revision and exams, a social life, training and competitions. The mental fatigue might come from having lots of work requiring high concentration or from having to deal with lots of things we find stressful. Mental fatigue is important in sport because studies have found it has a big impact on our performance. It slows us down, makes decisions tricky and creates a situation where our efforts feel harder. The effects have been found across a range of sports including cycling, running, football, swimming and table tennis.

In lots of sports athletes will have a bit of a physical taper before their competition to let their body rest and get stronger. We need to do this mentally too. Ideally, we avoid things which feel like they stretch our brain too much and we don't schedule stressful activities before a big competition. Sometimes this is unavoidable – such as when big exams are taking place at the same time as a key sporting competition so at that point you may need to lower your expectations for those competitions.

Expect tough times

Sport is supposed to be difficult at times. If it wasn't difficult we wouldn't get the same level of satisfaction from it. But it is natural to try to avoid that discomfort or those unpleasant feelings. Researchers have found that the best way to deal with those feelings is to accept, and expect them. When we know they are unavoidable we can cope much better and so everything doesn't feel so hard.

Elite Insight: Marilyn Okoro (track running): I think training always needs to be enjoyed. Of course it is going to hurt but once you know why you are doing it then you want to put yourself through that anyway because then you can race well.

When we expect tough times our perception of effort falls and so our effort levels can pick up. The phrase that is sometimes used is 'Brace yourself'. Expecting what is to come makes it feel so much more manageable. The more you try to control and resist these difficult moments the worse you will feel so expecting and accepting that tricky times are coming should help you cope and perform better.

Smiling

Smiling sounds silly, right? How does grinning our way through a competition make it feel easier? The jury is out on why, but researchers have found that it can work. They have found that smiling in competition not only reduces the feeling of effort you are putting in but that it can also increase your positive thoughts, relax your emotional state and in some sports improve performance indicators. The suggestion is that smiling makes us think what we have coming up isn't so hard.

It isn't just smiling to ourselves which is helpful. Having other people smile at us helps too. An experiment saw cyclists being asked to cycle until they felt they could absolutely do no more. Some of the riders had happy faces flashed at them (too fast to be aware of it) on their screens and some had grumpy faces flashed. Those seeing the smiles were able to cycle 12% longer than those who saw scowls and they felt the effort they needed to put in was less.

To use this knowledge in competition you can firstly smile when you feel you are struggling to give yourself a personal boost and secondly, hunt out those smiling in the crowd watching to suck up the power of their smiles.

Distraction

Some sports require solid concentration for up to 90 minutes. When this is the case we can't distract ourselves to make it feel easier. But some other sports offer the opportunity to switch off and on again and that 'off' time can be used to distract yourself from how you are feeling during the competition. You are purposefully interrupting that message which is going from your body trying to tell your brain you are uncomfortable and want to stop so that your brain doesn't hear it.

If you are competing in endurance sports like long-distance running or open-water swimming where you are competing for a really long time and don't need to be focusing for safety, or sports like golf or cricket where you will be out on the field of play for hours but only need to concentrate for minutes at a time, then mentally focusing on something completely unrelated to how your body is feeling at that moment is helpful. It will make the time go faster, reduce your boredom levels and ensure you get to the end of your competition without dropping out. It keeps your mind off the effort your body is having to put in and so makes your mind ignore some of the exertion your body is dealing with. It is worth saying that – while it is handy to keep you going – distraction is not a great strategy if you are focused on pure performance. A study of the US Olympic Marathon trial contestants found the highest finishers actually sucked up the pain and actively focused on how their bodies were feeling rather than distracting themselves from the discomfort.

There are lots of ways we can distract ourselves momentarily. Marathon runners are full of ideas for this as they get so much time to practise. Paula Radcliffe has talked about how she counts 3 times to 100 each mile as it helps her focus on that moment of the race and not how she is feeling. The rower Cath Bishop (who we met in Chapter 1) used to count backwards from 100 in German on her long ergo training sessions to reduce the boredom (and get in extra language practice). You need to find your own 'go to' method but some athletes try:

- Doing maths and equations in their heads about the distance or time left till the finish.

- Counting how many other athletes they overtake or see around them.

- Writing a competition report in their head.

- Thanking every volunteer or marshal.
- Planning their post-competition treat.
- Chatting to someone else nearby.
- Creating a competition in their head for the best banner or supporters sign spotted.

A motivational mantra

We all have an internal chatter echoing inside our heads. That chatter can have a really strong influence on our behaviours, our confidence, how motivated we are and how well we focus and perform. When we are in control of that chatter it can be brilliantly helpful and increase our chance of success. When that chatter feels out of control it can be incredibly unhelpful and destroy all the hard work we have put into our sport.

There are a number of different types of head chatter but the research into the theory behind it shows that the positive and helpful head chatter increases how long we can keep going for, helps us be excited about a competition (rather than being threatened by it) and improves our performance – both mentally and physically.

One type of head chatter that is brilliant at reducing the feeling of effort we are having to put in is a motivational mantra. It is a short phrase that is focused on helping your mind to stay motivated on either achieving your goal or staying true to your purpose for competing. You repeat it over and over again in your head at any point in your event when you start to struggle. This could be before the whistle goes to begin, when worrying about a poor score, when you start to doubt yourself or are trying to push harder than what feels comfortable.

Elite Insight: Cath Bishop (rowing): Our mantra was 'What's possible'. We said let's not focus on what isn't working or what is wrong but let's focus on what is possible; what is possible with the time we have got left, with the challenges we have got, the things we can't control; 'what is possible'. It is hopeful, it helps focus your mind.

Activity: Write your motivational mantra

A motivational mantra works best when it is really personal to you. Ideally it will give you a really powerful kick up the bum to work harder. It should be:

- Positive

- Purposeful

- Memorable

- Short

- Make you a little bit emotional

My motivational mantra is:

Rafael Nadal (tennis) in his book *Rafa* talks of how he used the phrase 'Yes we can'. His coach would tell him, "At every change over repeat it to yourself because you know what? The truth is you can do it. What you never allow yourself is to fail because of a loss of will."

SUCCESS STORY: DAME SARAH STOREY

Dame Sarah Storey began her professional sporting career as a swimmer. After winning six world championships and five Paralympic medals she switched sport to cycling. In cycling she has been the British track champion in the able-bodied category 6 times, para-cycling world champion 23 times on the track and 16 times on the road and won another 9 Paralympic titles. She is the most successful female British Paralympian of all time. She continues to race and, of course, win.

As an athlete your job is to ignore all the media chat and focus on what you can control. You know you can always go somewhere better, faster, more streamlined whatever it might be. It is never comfortable. I'm out of my comfort zone all the time. As a professional athlete you are always outside of your comfort zone otherwise you are not doing it right. I think if you were in your comfort zone it would be boring, and hard to perform because you are constantly having to make good decisions under pressure. I can feel confident but I will always feel out of my comfort zone even with confidence.

I think I am a bit sadistic. I don't mind it feeling uncomfortable. It is part of the process. A lot of athletes talk about the importance of getting comfortable with the uncomfortable and enjoying that is part of becoming better. There is never going to be a point where you are not learning or not being out of your comfort zone so I think for me that is part of that process and I enjoy that process of challenging myself.

You can't always control things, in both life and sport it is not going to go the way you expect it to and that is a really tough process to go through. I think it is something you learn in your teenage years. I don't think you can ever take anything for granted. Everybody else is working towards being the best they can be as well which may mean at some point they are improving faster than you expected, something you can't control. It is about accepting you can control your own change and the fact that nothing stays the same for long. Anyone who tries to find a comfortable position in sport is probably going to disappoint themselves because that is one of the beauties of sport – it is not comfortable but you learn to live with that discomfort.

You have to learn to step back on and focus on your own performance all of the time. I think for me, as a younger swimmer going into my teenage years (before I discovered the Paralympics) I wasn't quite good enough as an able bodied swimmer and so I just focused on my own performances all of the time so I would do personal best times. That was obviously the right approach to take in international sports because it massively takes the pressure off when everybody talks about gold medals and the outcome and you are very much focused on the process.

I have often acted braver than I felt. I think there are two types of athletes; those who have the need to achieve and those who have the need to avoid failure. I have always considered myself a 'need to achieve' and I think that is the bravery part, not being afraid to fail because failure is another opportunity to learn and do it differently next time.

There are some scary things in cycling, like descending. In training it is absolutely not worth taking the risk. If the road is closed and you know there is absolutely nothing coming the other way then you can break down the descent and the corners. In Rio Paralympics there was a fairly technical descent for the road race and I rode it multiple times steady because it was an open road. I didn't get the chance to ride it closed but I made all the mental notes of how I would ride it closed.

I think that taking the logical approach to the things that are concerning you means you can be sure that you have made the right decision. And then you know you have done everything in your power to make the right decision. If it doesn't go well on the day and you end up crashing then you'll learn from that for the next time. It is about utilising that logical process which is the same for any fear you have to overcome.

I'm still motivated to race because I like that sense of being out of my comfort zone still. I am comfortable with the uncomfortable. I still like finding that next best performance, that next opportunity to go better, faster, learn something, so I think that being comfortable with the uncomfortable probably allows you to go on for longer because you are never looking for something that is comfortable.

CHAPTER 4

I can be confident

Confidence separates the successful from the unsuccessful. So much so that when 300 Olympic and 6000 amateur athletes were asked their thoughts on the most influential element of success in sport, confidence came out on top. It is essential if you want to make the most of your time in sport.

Confidence is a magical mix of self-belief and positivity that gives us that feeling that we can achieve what we set out to do. It influences how we think, feel and behave so that when we have high levels of it, it reduces the fear we might get ahead of competition so we can focus on executing our skills excellently.

Ninety per cent of Olympians report having a very high level of confidence and when a whole bunch of studies on confidence were dissected, they found a clear relationship between confidence and performance. So, it seems to be a key characteristic of athletes. It may be that those without high levels of confidence already dropped out of sport before reaching the elite levels as studies have found that confident athletes are less likely to dropout and so tend to play their sport for longer.

The positive news is that confidence isn't restricted and that we can all grow the amount we have. There are loads of different strategies we can use to increase the amount of confidence we have and the number of places we get it from.

So why does confidence help us in competitions?

Sporting confidence gives us a ton of benefits. It makes us more resilient so we bounce back from tricky situations and makes us mentally stronger so we can focus on executing our sporting skills. It can also help us stay calm and relaxed under pressure as we feel like everything is under control. This calmness means our mind has time to focus on doing the good stuff which will help us succeed – like decent competition strategies, bravery to take on new challenges, more commitment – and simply makes everything feel a bit easier.

HOW CONFIDENT ARE YOU

As confidence has such a strong influence over our success in sport it is helpful to measure it.

Activity: Find your sporting confidence level

Tick the box for each question ...	Very rarely	A little	Sometimes	Quite often	Always
I know how to do the techniques required in my sport					
I am good at making decisions in competition					
I can perform under pressure					
I know which tactics to use in my sport					
I have the ability to be consistently successful in my sport					
I think fast and effectively during competition					
I know I can meet the challenges of competition					

Tick the box for each question ...	Very rarely	A little	Sometimes	Quite often	Always
I can succeed even when the risks are high					
I am able to squash my self-doubt					
I can do well even if everything seems stacked against me					
I am good at bouncing back from setbacks					

Low confidence: If you have lots of crosses in the 'very rarely' and 'a little' boxes then you are likely to be low in confidence. This means that you might doubt yourself which harms your performance. You might feel you often do better in training than in competition. You might hesitate over making decisions, even if deep down you know what you should do. You might find yourself focusing on your weaknesses instead of your strengths. When you have low confidence your mind is so busy fighting off anxiety, nerves and negative thoughts that you don't have space to perform at your best. This feels horrible and so to protect yourself, you may pull back from putting in the right effort level which can leave you feel frustrated and stop you from getting the results or success you deserve.

Elite Insight: Marilyn Okoro (track runner): My confidence has been pretty up and down. Secure, then a knock, then secure, then on the elite stage it was knocked again because I realised people aren't just watching my running and critiquing that, they are critiquing what I look like and how that doesn't fit in with the 800m. As long as I was running well I thought I could handle anything but as soon as you have the injury or knock in confidence you start to spiral.

<u>Medium confidence</u>: If you have ticked a mixture of 'a little', 'sometimes' and 'quite often' then you still need to boost your confidence. You will really want to focus on building up your robust sources of confidence (mastery and preparation – covered on page 88) so that you can be consistently confident and not like you are on a bit of a rollercoaster with your sport – up and down and regularly feeling wobbly.

<u>Optimal confidence</u>: If you have a good mix of 'quite often' and 'always' boxes then you probably have a good level of confidence. This is where you believe your goals are reachable but will still do everything possible to make them happen. You trust in the training you have put both your body and brain through and manage any doubts productively. While the confidence won't completely stop any pre-competition nerves, it can act as a bit of a buffer, so you get optimal activation levels and have the capacity to prepare well and focus on what is important.

<u>Over confidence</u>: If you ticked mainly 'always' then you will have a high level of confidence – but is it actually too high? While it sounds brilliant to have super high confidence it can make you a little complacent, stop you working as hard as you need to or mean you miss key elements of preparation suggesting you don't have the hunger that a small dose of self-doubt provides. This lack of growth can reduce mastery and your long-term chances of success.

Elite Insight: Jonny Wilkinson (rugby): A thin line separates self-belief from arrogance. I have never been able to condone arrogant behaviour in sport. Nothing fires up opposition teams more than when they can sense disrespect expressed in terms of hugely over shored and brash views.

FAKING CONFIDENCE

Confidence is best when it is real. But it does take a while to grow so, in the meantime, as our thoughts, feelings and behaviours all feed off each other, if we behave as if we are confident, we can start to feel more confident. This 'fake it till you make it' idea sounds rather cheesy but scientists have found it is really effective. Think of it as, 'if you are in scary place – pretend to be a scary person'. There are two ways to do it.

The first way works in a similar way to a placebo, where your coach or parents manipulate your performance data so you feel like you are performing well and the expectations that come from this influence your performance. A study of weightlifters highlighted this when they found that when the athletes were deliberately lied to about how much weight they had lifted their confidence rose and they could lift increasingly heavier weights.

The second way is to act confident. Even when you don't feel like it. Our brain processes images 60,000 times faster than it does words and 50–70% of our communication is non-verbal so our body language and the clothes we wear help us seem more powerful to ourselves and to our competitors. This gives us a performance advantage and reduces our stress levels. We can start by using a power pose.

Activity: Power pose

Your power pose should see you with:

- Your head held high
- Chest forward
- Shoulders back and down

- Thinking tall and wide
- Your feet apart and firmly placed on the ground

You need to practise this regularly until the stance feels natural.

Once you have your pose nailed you can think about the kit you wear to compete. Sometimes we get no choice. If we are in a team and there is a uniform we follow the rules. But if you get any freedom over what you wear then make it a powerful colour.

Champions often wear red. Red is considered to be powerful, dominant and physical and has been found to influence motivation. When they ran some research at the 2004 Athens Olympics they looked at the combat sport athletes who are randomly assigned either a blue or red uniform. Those wearing red strips won significantly more often than those wearing blue. Another study that same year, looking football teams at the 2004 European Championships, also found those teams wearing red won more than they statistically should have done.

GOLD STANDARD CONFIDENCE

Our confidence is influenced by some elements we can't control – our age, gender, personality, the motivational climate of the sport we compete in and the culture of the clubs we compete for. Studies have shown these are pretty much ingrained. But positively there are lots of things we can do to maximise our confidence. When we understand the different places we can get confidence from we can learn ways to boost our own levels of confidence.

Of all the different ways we can build our confidence two of them – mastery and preparation – are super robust so that even if you have a bad couple of weeks or a dive in performance you can still keep going. Mastery and preparation give you both physical and mental evidence that you can do whatever is necessary in the competition ahead making you feel a little bit invincible. This is gold standard confidence.

MASTERY

Knowing you have already achieved something or mastered the skills needed is an awesome source of confidence. It is the difference between a gymnast nervously standing at the edge of the mat about to try their hardest tumble in the routine knowing they have never pulled it together in training or standing there feeling pumped knowing they managed it five times in a row in their last session.

Always focusing on mastery instead of outcomes helps us get this confidence as it means we take our training and practice sessions seriously and work hard to continually improve. It gives a great foundation for all the other sources of confidence to be built on as it gives you clear evidence you can achieve your goals. The more you do this the better you get and so your confidence grows which allows you to stretch your comfort zone and keep trying things which are slightly harder. It means you are always developing and improving.

As well as focusing on mastery in training and doing lots of practice we can log what we do in our training diaries. This helps our efforts stick in our memory and gives us a physical place where evidence for why we should be confident is clearly captured. Another way to capture that evidence is in a 'confidence jar'.

Activity: Confidence jar

We tend to remember negative things much more than positive ones. In fact, our brain is designed to do so to keep us safe. Yet when we have evidence of our previous performances and skills we can feel confident that we have those superpowers ready to use when the time comes. Having a list or a jar full of reminders of these great performances and skills can be really helpful when having a bad day because having good things to remember about ourselves makes us perform better.

You need to get a jar (anything jam jar sized or smaller is great) and 25 thin strips of paper. You need to write on the strips:

- Achievements you are really proud of
- Setbacks you handled well
- Compliments you have received from others that made you feel good
- Challenges you have overcome
- Tricky skills you have learnt

Keep your jar in your kit bag or in your room and add to it everytime you notice something else you do well or something you achieve that you are proud of. Leaving it out to see means if you start getting nervous or if you are finding your confidence has taken a dip you just grab it and read through your skills and success. You can be reminded, in your own writing and words, all the reasons you have to be confident. You can also take your jar away with you to competitions so you have continual evidence of all the times previously when you have overcome fears and reached your goals.

PREPARATION

The other really robust way of building confidence is being brilliantly prepared. The more you have put into a competition or challenge, the more confident you can feel about nailing it and the less you should fear it. This means you need to really focus on covering your preparation from every angle including physical training, skills development, potential tactics and mental practice. You also need to consider the logistics of the event so you are signed up to it before deadline, arrive with plenty of time, have all the right kit with you and warm up in a way that helps your body and mind. When you are fully physically, skilfully, logistically and mentally prepared nothing is left to chance and so you should have a great source of confidence. Your training diary comes in handy here as it is a great way of capturing your preparation. Reading through it ahead of competition helps you see just how much preparation you did in the build-up.

If you want some additional preparation, imagery is a brilliant skill we can learn.

Activity: Imagery

Our brains are amazing. We don't even need to physically do something for our brain to recognise it, build new connections and make it feel like we have achieved it. We do still have to do some physical training (it doesn't get us out of hard practice) but by visualising success or skills in our sport well enough we can supplement our physical practice without risking the injury or fatigue we get when we push too far. It helps us feel familiar with what is ahead and makes us feel really well prepared for difficult situations we might come up against in competition.

> Elite Insight: Michael Phelps (swimming): I can visualise how I want the perfect race to go. I can see the start, the strokes, the walls, the turns, the finish, the strategy, all of it. … I can vividly see incredible detail, down even to the wake behind me. It's my imagination at work, and I have a big imagination. Visualising like this is like programming a race in my head, and that programming sometimes seems to make it happen just as I had imagined it.

As Phelps shows, imagery isn't just daydreaming. Imagery is much more focused. You do it with a specific purpose in mind. It can be good to think of it like a mental rehearsal where you can practise all the things you are worried about (and make them go well) so your brain learns what to do, rather than what not to do.

We can use it at any point – in the car on the way to a competition, in the changing room, during a break in training or at home in bed. It can work either directly by improving your skills or strategies or indirectly by boosting your motivation, helping you ramp up or dial down your activation levels, increasing your self-confidence or helping you prepare yourself for a particular situation that regularly makes you nervous.

To make it really effective we don't just use images in our heads. We use all our senses, as the more vivid and realistic the images are the more likely our brain is to interpret them as similar to the actual event.

> Elite Insight: Deena Kastor (running): Every afternoon for three months before the championships I ran through a race scenario. I put Joga by Björk on the stereo, lay on my bed, and closed my eyes. The moment I heard the slow and dramatic instrumental opening, the heightened feel of the race came to me. I watched myself pin on my bib number and tie my shoes. … I lined up at the front. Right toes on the line, knee bent, left arm crooked in front, the gun fired and I flew.

Before you start your imagery you need to decide what you want to get out of it. There are five options to pick from:

1. To rehearse competition plans or strategies.
2. To rehearse specific sports skills.
3. To dial down anxiety or psych up before an event.
4. To feel in control, focused or mentally tough.
5. To boost motivation to achieve your goal.

Once you have picked your purpose you need to write your script. Get all Hollywood here. Go all out. Make it as realistic as possible so you create rich and realistic images.

1. Describe the situation you will imagine:
2. What will you be able to see:
3. What can you hear:

4. What can you feel in your hands or on your skin:
5. What can you taste:
6. What can you smell:

Then mix it all together until it feels like you have a realistic script.

The finished script should take about 2–3 minutes to read out. Record it on your phone and listen to it regularly. As your imagery skills get better your images should get clearer and more controlled so you can either make new scripts which are longer or start to use imagery without needing a script. Once you get really good at imagery you no longer need a script and should be able to do it from anywhere. This means instead of mindlessly scrolling through social media when on the bus or waiting for someone you can visualise your successful performances.

Some people like to do imagery when physically practising their sport – this can work well in controllable sports such as rowing or cycling where you can be on a Concept 2 or an indoor bike. For most sports though it is safer and more effective to do your imagery sitting down.

Close your eyes. Start to notice your breathing. Slow your breathing right down until you feel calm and focused. Then listen to your recorded script.

Here is an example script for a swimmer who wants to stay focused and ignore all distractions throughout their 50 metre freestyle competition:

I enter the pool area. I take a deep breath and the smell of the chlorine hits me. I can feel it in my throat. It is the smell of racing. I scan the pool. Empty right now. Water smooth. Super clean.

I switch off my music and my ears tune into the poolside atmosphere. It is noisy. There are lots of supporters up in the stands. Friends and family all come to cheer. I can make out my mum and dad's voices. They are always loud. I love it. Makes me feel really special.

They call our race. I take my headphones off and into my bag. I put my towel on top. I jump up and down to warm my legs. I swing my arms to get my blood pumping. I feel ready.

I check my hat and tighten my goggles. I take a long deep breath and walk over to the edge of the pool. I look up and down my lane. This is going to be exciting. I have trained so hard for this race and today I get to make the magic happen.

I climb onto my starting block. I roll my neck to remove any tightness. It feels satisfying. I visualise a pair of curtains around the pool and in my mind I draw them shut so all I can see is my lane. No noise from the crowd, no competitors in other lanes, no splashing. Just me and my lane ahead of me.

I hear the starter. On your marks. ... I bend down into my starting position, weight on the front foot. I am ready for action. I am ready to go fast. I hear the beep and dive neatly into the water. I feel strong and powerful. My kick pushes me back to the surface and I am away. I begin to move my arms. Long, powerful, strong strokes. I'm gliding through the water. I can feel the water but I'm sliding through it. As I take a breath I can hear the roar of the crowds and it fuels me. It feeds my strength. I am getting stronger and stronger with each stroke. I know there are swimmers either side but they don't bother me. All I am focused on is myself and my stroke. Moving as powerfully as I can. Power will bring speed.

I can see the cross under the water and it is time to flip. The wall approaches quickly. That is a great sign. I start the turn. I throw my legs over my head and push off hard. A butterfly kick and I'm streamlined and make into my rhythm. I know my body will be feeling tired right now so I attack harder. I concentrate on getting the most distance out of each stroke. If I focus on each individual stroke I'll show my power. That is enough for me. Those endurance sessions are kicking in and I'm glad I did them – I am strong. I'm speeding up. I've got enough left to give. I'm propelling myself forward and I'm close. Two more strokes. One more stroke. A final kick and I surge forward and touch the wall. A moment of fuzziness and everything comes flooding back. The noise, the smell, the feel of the water. I don't need to look at the scoreboard. I can hear from the crowd I've done well. Better than well in fact. I'm so proud of myself.

BUILDING UP CONFIDENCE

As well as the two elements of gold standard confidence there are lots of other ways we can get confidence. Overall, we are looking for you to be confident in three areas:

- That you can make the right decisions
- That you have done the right physical training and learning
- That you believe you can bounce back from setbacks

From our friends or rivals

We might get told that we should be really inspired by seeing our favourite pro athletes competing but they are usually such a long way from our current success levels that while they are fun to watch they are not inspirational. Where we can get strong levels of confidence though is from watching other athletes who are a little bit like us. It is called 'vicarious confidence'. It might be a teammate or even a rival but they show us what is possible if we get our heads down and work hard. They make us start to believe that if they can do it then so can I.

When Michael Phelps saw an edition of Swimming World where a rival was the front cover and had a centrefold he pulled out the centrefold of his rival and put it up on the wall above his bed. "Every morning the first thing I'd see when I woke up was that photo. Every morning that photo was a kick in the backside. It drove me. It pushed me", he has written.

Confidence question: The person I get my vicarious confidence from is:

Confidence question: They inspire me because:

Others believing in us

When other people show they have faith in our abilities and efforts it gives a real boost to our confidence. A study looking at teachers found that when they were told specific students were clever those students were given lots more attention and encouragement. This was reflected in their grades and they ended up matching their 'clever' label – even though they had never been any different originally and the teachers had been tricked.

Confidence question: The people who believe in me and encourage me are:

Having a great coach

If we really respect our coach, trust in their methods and knowledge and feel they have our best intentions at heart then that can give us a great amount of confidence. The issue to remember with this is that coaching relationships do change. Sometimes we grow out of the coach we have and other times they or we move, so while it can really help at times it is not always a reliable source of confidence.

Confidence question: A coach I work with that I really trust and respect is:

Feeling at home

The environment we train in is really important. If it feels familiar and we are comfortable there, with both the physical place and the other athletes then you will be able to relax into training and competition without feeling the need to be on edge. This can give you a great deal of confidence. You are one of the gang.

Confidence question: I feel comfortable when I am ...

Social support

Having support from the people who are important to us is a great source of confidence. It could be your friends, family, club mates or coach. Feeling that we are well supported and have people to go to whenever we need it, and will like us even if we weren't an athlete, is priceless. Occasionally this support can feel a bit like an expectation and adds pressure rather than confidence so if this happens train your supporters to focus on the efforts you are putting into your sport rather than the outcomes so they feel like a help rather than a hindrance.

Confidence question: My three biggest fans are:

1:

2:

3:

STRENGTH SPOTTING

Now that we know where we get our personal confidence from we can identify our specific strengths so we can pull real, usable confidence from them to help us achieve our goals. Highlighting our own strengths can be really hard as we get told to be modest and humble and that no one likes those with 'big heads' but we have to put our humility to one side when we want to build up our sporting confidence. It is super important as while there are hundreds of good athletes, your strengths are what will help you stand out as excellent.

Identifying them when calm and outside of a competition environment is good because our memories are not always reliable, especially in the heat of the moment, and our brains are wired with a number of biases which help keep us safe but tend to mean we remember negatives much more than our positives. Pushing forward our positives stops us inadvertently from seeing things from the dark side, maximises our motivation and builds our confidence, showing us exactly what we have within us that helps us perform well. One way to do this is to create your 'Stars in the Dark'.

Activity: Stars in the dark.

We are looking to fill in the 10 stars. This means finding two strengths in each area:

- Fitness (these could be things like good endurance, great pace, speedy direction changes, fast feet)

- Strategy/tactics (like being quick to figure out opponents, good mid-match analysis, ability to keep calm, can easily see opportunities, well-practised set pieces)

- Skills (very personal to your sport but might be things like strong ground stokes, great tackling, ball accuracy, drive)

- Mindset (the types of approach or attitude you bring to a competition or training)

- Support (the specific people who give you great support and encouragement)

It can feel really uncomfortable blowing our own trumpet but you will have to put aside any humility to find your strengths. You don't need to worry about seeming arrogant – no one else will see your answers – but you need to be honest if this is to work for you.

If you struggle to come up with your strengths there are a number of places to go hunting:

1. Your training diary – read through and see where you tend to shine.
2. Consider other areas of your life (like school or other hobbies) to see if there are any transferable strengths.
3. Ask your coach what they would see as your strengths.
4. Ask your parents or caregivers.
5. Finally, if you feel brave enough, ask your friends and teammates. This won't just give you nice things to write on your stars but knowing others have recognised great stuff in you is confidence boosting in itself.

MAINTAINING CONFIDENCE

Mastery and preparation are brilliant for robust confidence. But most other types of confidence are quite fragile so we need to nurture them. We can think of confidence like a flower; when it is well cared for it looks strong and beautiful but to stay that way it needs watering and protecting from weeds. One way to do this is to remind ourselves we have the skills and experience we need and that we are fully prepared for the competition ahead. We can do this through a confidence booster.

Activity: Confidence booster

A confidence booster can help you reduce nerves and gives you a visual reminder of the efforts you have put in ahead of your competition. It should give you reassurance and lots of positive things to remember if you find your confidence lacking.

Goal for the competition (ideally something within your control)	Your motivational mantra (Chapter 3) you will use if it gets tough
Three strengths you will use in the competition 1. 2. 3.	Three key sessions you completed in your build-up 1. 2. 3.
I deserve to be confident because …	

We should create our confidence booster a few days before each event. Looking through your training diary will give you lots of the information you need to create it. Once filled in, keeping it in your wallet or kit bag means when you find the nerves sneaking in, you have to pull it out, read through it and know that you deserve to be confident and achieve your goal.

SUCCESS STORY: EMMA WIGGS

Emma Wiggs MBE has excelled in two sports: sitting volleyball and now canoeing. She took up sitting volleyball after attending a talent identification day and quickly made it onto the GB Team, competing at the 2012 London Paralympics. She then switched to canoeing and put her teaching career on hold to become a full-time athlete. The trade-off worked and she has since won eight world championship titles and the gold medal at the 2016 Rio Paralympics.

I sometimes really struggle with confidence and belief. I was unbeaten for the first six years of my career and yet I never lined up expecting to win. But I am confident that I can train harder than most people, I can make good decisions, I can eat more cottage cheese than anyone else, I can go to bed earlier than anyone else. I think those kind of things help confidence rather than thinking I am amazing and I can win every race. My potential lack of confidence means I leave no stone unturned and that then gives me huge confidence to line up knowing I have done everything I could, without any regrets.

I am a really big planner and I would urge any teenage athlete to look at their approach to planning and process because I take huge confidence from understanding that plan and the process we are going through. It gives me confidence to ask questions and to understand why we are doing something. I think it is important to question, to get information and more understanding. I can take confidence from that information and I can take reassurance and empowerment from knowing the answers to my questions.

As I have got a bit older I realise the extra win is in asking those questions and being confident in asking them so you actually engage more. I shouldn't be as fast as I am in a boat, because of my level of disability and my age, so something sets me apart. I think it is because I am a student of my sport. I want to understand it. I want to ask questions and I want to take confidence from knowing I am learning and I am checking and I am challenging what we are doing. Everyone can train. Everyone can do the exercises they are told to do. If you are a student of your sport and focusing on what you are doing then that might mean you train slightly harder which might give you the edge. And if you feel you are in control of what you are doing maybe you're a bit less worried about everybody else which might give you another edge.

A couple of times I've used an alter ego so on race day I will put on my superhero pants and think I am gonna go out and be the person no-one expects me to be. It means on race day you are quietly, confidently just getting on with your stuff, not letting those doubts creep in to be verbalized. If I was a superhero I wouldn't say to a team mate or competitor 'I am tired and I've got a bit of a neck injury'. I would just say 'Have a good race' and just act my way out.

I'm a really strong fan of imagery. I find it a really strong technique and I think it is really underused. It is so varied, you can do so many different types. I do quite a lot of bad weather visualisation because that is where I am lowest in confidence. And it isn't about the result. I don't put the result into my visualisation anywhere. It is about how I am feeling and my technique and what my strategy is. I make the boat feel powerful. I find doing it in moments of training useful. I have done some visualisations recorded as voice memos on my phone and got into a habit of listening of them.

I probably rely quite heavily on the people in my immediate support team for confidence. We are an individual sport but when the rest of the team are doing well it is very powerful.

CHAPTER 5

I can control my emotions

When we compete we can feel under the microscope. Watched. Judged. Discussed. Analysed. It can be horrible. We know what we are capable of. We know what we would like to achieve and each time things don't go our way our temper gets frayed. Sometimes it might get out of hand.

We all remember the players who lob their tennis racquet across the court with frustration, kick the football off the pitch in anger or throw their bike down the side of a mountain (and then see them realise what they have done and have to go scampering off down the side to get it). We do not want to be that athlete. It does your reputation no good and gives your competitors an easy way to get ahead: they'll purposefully wind you up and let you self-destruct. The emotions bubbling up show you care. They show you are invested. But they need to be kept under control if you are to make a success of your sport.

The first step is to know what is likely to tip our emotions over the edge. What is sitting deep in our brain, pushing our anxieties to the edge? If we can get them out of our head and onto a page we can free up some of our brain before we head into our event. Reading a list of these things means you sometimes see the fear isn't as bad as we have built it up to be and if it is sitting there in front of us we can prepare better, so we expect it to happen rather than snapping with stress when it occurs. It has been found to work well in schools. In the 15 minutes before a maths exam, researchers asked one group of students to sit and wait and another group to write about the anxiety they were feeling. The group who wrote down their fears got significantly better marks in the exam than their 'sit and wait' friends. We call it a 'Brain Drain' and we can use this tactic for our sport too.

Activity: Brain drain

This sheet is to be filled in before you compete. It should only take a couple of minutes and you can even incorporate it into your pre-performance routine that you developed in Chapter 2. The idea is to write down absolutely anything you are worried about. No one ever needs to know what you write. It is not for sharing with your coach or parents. In fact you can throw it away before you compete. It is the action of writing it that helps – getting the fears out of your head and onto the paper.

Area	Fears	Anything I can do ahead of starting
Equipment		
My ability		
Other competitors		
The outcome		
Technique or skills		
Others' opinions		
Weather		
Venue/course/pitch/court		

THE CAUSES OF OUT-OF-CONTROL EMOTIONS

Getting our fears out of our heads can help us to respond better to the scary stuff when it does happen. But we are too complex for this to fix all our worries or our mid-competition responses. The beauty of us as humans is that we are all unique with so many different elements dictating our behaviours, attitudes and thoughts. What we put into our sport will be a mixture of our personality traits and preferences, the different expectations upon us, our genes, training history, our environment and our culture. They all impact our emotional response in sport.

> Elite Insight: Kelly Smith (football): I have been sent off for some stupid things, and that's because I haven't been able to keep my cool in certain situations.

Learning to control our emotional response will firstly come from a real understanding of what triggers us to lose control. When we understand ourselves better it is easier to spot our risk factors: Do we have lots of negative head chatter taking place? Are we a perfectionist? Do we lack confidence? Do we constantly fear failure? Do we get frustrated when plans change? To understand why those triggers are important we firstly need to understand what is going on in our brain when all of this happens.

OUR BRAINS DURING COMPETITION

In Chapter 2 we worked on how to ramp up or dial down our activation levels so we can get the right mindset ahead of competition. This is possible because we can usually create a calm(ish) environment to do this before competition.

Elite Insight: Jonny Brownlee: There's the balance in your mental approach. You need to be alert, but you can't cross over into being tense.

What happens though when we over-activate and feel that the pressure and nerves have become too intense once the competition has started? We may become hyperactive, overly nervous, or frustrated; lose our tempter quickly and make rubbish decisions under pressure. It makes us emotionally fragile and our performance can nosedive.

It all comes down to which part of our brain is in charge.

A really nice way to understand it comes from Professor Steve Peters whose book *The Chimp Paradox* is used by lots of athletes to figure out how to remain calmer and cope better when under pressure in competition.

Our brains are super complex. Even though they only weigh 1.4 kg, our brains contain 86 billion neurons. These neurons make continuous connections and reconnections and can even regenerate. Some of the structures are shaped by our genes but more are shaped by our experiences – this is important when it comes to our behaviours. For two key behaviours – emotional regulation and decision-making – three areas are vital for us to know about. Officially they are known as parietal region, prefrontal cortex and amygdala. Peters however helps us remember them as our computer, human and chimp. When we understand how they work, we can work with them to develop helpful sporting behaviours.

Our 'computer' acts like a storage unit holding all our values, memories, experiences and habits. It has the ability to work without us realising it, making lots of decisions based on pre-programmed thoughts and behaviours. This is really handy because we need to make up to 35,000 decisions a day and if we had to think about each of them we'd never get anything done. Having our computer work away in the background, making these unconscious decisions for us automatically means we get lots of headspace left over for the other decisions and actions which require more strategy or tactical knowledge.

Our 'human' is our rational and sensible part of our brain. When a problem or issue comes our way that needs a more considered decision, we humans sort through its library for the relevant facts and knowledge to make a good quality decision. All good.

But we also have one other area: our chimp. And it is our chimp who can cause chaos.

Our chimp is hyper responsive to threat. It is basically an alarm system. When something could harm us it starts shouting and screaming. This is incredibly helpful when it is something physical, like being followed too closely when out walking or when you are about to cycle down a mountain really fast. The problem is most of us have pretty safe lives now and the harms we fear don't come from physical threats but threats to our ego and to our sense of who we are as a person. Our chimp is pretty rubbish at distinguishing a physical threat from an ego-driven one so when something looks like it could threaten our ego, making us look silly, or like a failure or screwing up something we have worked really hard to achieve, then our chimp gets switched on.

The snooker player Ronnie O'Sullivan worked with Professor Peters when he was struggling with his anxiety and he used his improved understanding of what was going on in his brain to help him win the 2012 World Championship. In his book *Running* he shares some of his diary entries when he was dealing with his chimp – here is one of them: "Got up. Felt like the chimp was at me. Telling me you're not consistent, that you're gonna start mistiming balls. I let him have his say and then said right now I'm going to give you some logic. I'm enjoying the game and I want to play I've been feeling really good about my game recently. I'm thinking a lot clearer." We can all think clearer when we understand our chimp.

GETTING TO KNOW OUR CHIMP

Our chimp is designed such that when it is triggered it directs our body to do one of three things: fight, flight or freeze. We each seem to have our own preference of 'go to' response.

Question: What is your preferred threat response?

Fight: You get really annoyed and aggressive or obviously frustrated in competition when things are not going your way or the event is not being run fairly. ☐

Flight: You are so scared of how you might perform before competitions that you would much prefer not to go and have to be bribed or coxed to go. ☐

Freeze: When you get to crucial parts of a competition you 'choke' and fall apart. ☐

This threat response is our base instinct. It needs to be speedy to protect us (in fact it works five times faster than our human) so it jumps very quickly to conclusions. It needs to be paranoid to ensure we are safe so it ends up making us pretty irrational. We can think of our chimp as emotional and impulsive. The decisions it makes are based not on evidence but on feelings. And when we are in a competition and how we feel about ourselves is tied up with the outcome of the competition it is little wonder our chimp comes out to play far too often. The bigger or more important the competition is to us, the more likely our chimp is to make an appearance.

Now that we know a bit about the chimp (and our human and computer) we can name them. This may feel a bit silly as it is part of you but by naming them you get to distance yourself a little from its tricky behaviours. It means you can stand back a little and observe how they are behaving, and how you would rather behave than feeling all caught up in the middle of it. Some people will name their chimp versions of their name, others names they like or dislike. My name is Josephine so

I call my computer Josephine, my human Josie and my chimp Jo (I hate being called Jo) so when I notice Jo coming out it feels easy to distance myself and have a word with her. I have heard some brilliant names for chimps over the years including Arnie (as they imagined their chimp looking like Arnold Schwarzenegger) and the names of their sporting enemies.

Question: My computer is called:

Question: My human is called:

Question: My chimp is called:

As we learnt in Chapter 2, when we switch into a threat mindset and our chimp comes out our bodies become flooded with cortisol and adrenaline which pushes our heart rate and breathing patterns up. Exactly the type of physical response you don't want mid competition. If you learn how to quieten your chimp and put your human back in charge you reduce the impact and quantity of these responses and so are more likely to make good decisions and perform well. First though, we need to know what triggers our chimp.

TRIGGERING OUR CHIMP

There are lots of things that will trigger our chimp. And what may trigger mine might be completely ignored by yours. The triggers will develop over time maybe because of your personality traits, a previous experience, specific types of people who wind you up or a sense of fairness that gets trampled all over.

Elite Insight: Dame Kelly Holmes (runner): I was thinking far too much about how I should be performing, worrying I should be fitter than I needed to be at that stage of the year. I was putting too much pressure on myself because it was an Olympic year, I ran erratically and was just not completely focused.

Some triggers are external and outside of our control, others are internal and so should feel like we are better able to control – and so we get even more frustrated when we can't. Two big triggers that many of us have are expectations and fear of failure.

Piling on the pressure

One of the biggest triggers for our chimp is expectation – both from ourselves and from others. It creates pressure which adds to the feeling of threat.

Some of these expectations come with the job. If you are a full-time professional athlete then the media and managers and fans will be talking about your form and fitness and their views will feel like they are being shoved in your face as you are asked about them in press conferences, see yourself discussed on social media or have managers or performance directors mention you in meetings.

Most of the time there is no malice behind the expectations. People think they are helping by telling you that you will 'do well', or you are 'a great athlete' or 'I just know you will win'. They don't realise that their words are adding a burden onto your shoulders, directing your focus towards the outcome and mean that if you lose not only do you feel rubbish for losing but you also feel you've failed to live up to their expectations.

While many comments are designed to make you feel better they can block fun, make you overthink, get you focusing on the outcome rather than the processes and cause you a big pile of stress. They can harm your performance because these expectations switch your focus from 'trying to do well' into 'trying not to lose'. Trying to win uses our human brain to work out logically 'what can I do to play better'. Trying not to lose feeds off your chimp brain where you start work out how to not mess up.

These expectations are a huge kick up the bum to our chimp. They wind it up and off it goes. Often causing havoc. Our chimp floods our body with cortisol and adrenaline, our stomach wants to empty so we can escape faster (which is why some people want to throw up with nerves and others are continually heading off to the toilet) and our muscles get tight.

Sometimes the expectations are not explicit, or even spoken about. We have put them in place because we know that people have spent lots of time helping us, or our parents have spent so much money on our sport, or lots of time driving us to training and competitions. These silent expectations sit in our brain ready to go off whenever we feel like we might let these people down. Other expectations come purely because we have an internal driver to do well. We know how much we want success. We know how hard we have worked and so it is only fair we should get the reward for that. We have set goals and we expect ourselves to meet them. The problem is these just become additional stressors and mid competition we really don't have the mental capacity to go to our usual coping mechanisms.

Fear of failure

Fear of failure takes many forms. It might be a fear of losing competitions, of others gossiping about how you have done, of embarrassing yourself, of letting teammates, coaches or family down or of not putting what you have practised into practice. It is likely to be worse if your motivation for your sport comes from outside of you. If you love playing and would play even if you were rubbish at it then failing will feel less important. If you love the status boost, the prizes or the social life that comes from competing then fear of failure might be far up on your radar.

Elite Insight: Jonny Wilkinson (rugby): I don't want to lose is not the same sort of thought as I want to win. The message that this focus emits is totally different. The first is almost a plea for mercy which gives away any power you have as you cry to be spared by chance, the latter is an eminently stronger more proactive intention which forces you to look inside and uncover the innate strength we all possess for making things happen. Fear is negative and inhibiting. Ambition is positive and motivating.

Fear of failure can be quite a driver for performance. It can push us to train harder, to practise more, to put in more effort in competitions and to take all the great advice offered to us. But it also pushes us to avoid tricky situations, stay in our comfort zone rather than getting brave and play not to lose, rather than to win. It will make us pretty average. And if you wanted to be average you wouldn't be reading this book.

Hunger

You might have heard of the word 'hangry'. It covers that emotion of being angry because you are hungry. It sounds like a made-up term but it is recognised and studied by scientists as it can have a big impact on us. It can certainly trigger our chimp as studies have seen when we have not eaten for a while we are more likely to be impulsive, aggressive, and irritable and to overreact.

Our body tells us we are hungry when our glucose (blood sugar) levels drop too low. When our blood sugar gets too low lots of hormones are set off, including cortisol (our stress hormone) and adrenaline. They are released into our bloodstream to help raise and rebalance our blood sugar. But, these are also the two chemicals which are set off by our chimp switching on when they respond to threat. And as we know it is a circular reaction. If our body is flooded with cortisol and adrenaline our brain reads that as being under threat, so reacts by releasing even more cortisol and adrenaline. Getting us into a threat state and releasing our chimp.

This doesn't happen to everyone though. Something makes it more likely. And that is being already stressed, being overly activated or being in a bad mood. A US study found these unpleasant situations make us focus on and respond to our hunger feelings more. If we are in a positive happy situation and feel hungry we will just plan our next snack. If we are feeling under stress or worried (as we might well be in a competition) then our hunger adds to our negative feelings and tips us over the edge into hanger and triggers our chimp.

Unfairness

Cheating is really tough to deal with in competition. For everyone. But if you have fairness or justice as a core value (more on these in Chapter 8) then a dodgy line call in tennis, someone tapping a golf ball out of the rough or an elbow in the ribs in football is likely to tip you over into anger. When we add in high stakes and a big impact on the potential outcome we find it isn't just that that competitor has been dishonest and behaved in a way that rocks your values but it is also that they are stealing potential success from you.

Studies have found that when we notice these moral violations (like cheating) we physically feel them in our head and face. Scans will show there are the areas which are highly activated. This, researchers have suggested, means we associate moral violations with high-level cognitive processing. And this is why their unjust behaviours will emotionally hijack you and kick your chimp into action. Then, while the cheater has moved on, our mind is stuck on how badly they cheated 5 minutes ago rather than focusing on how to beat them right now. We end up sacrificing our own performance because the indignation at how others have behaved has taken over our mental focus.

Question: What triggers my chimp?

1.

2.

3.

Now that you have your worries written down and you know what sets your chimp off you can learn how to change the conversations in our head so we reduce the number of times our chimp is triggered.

CHANGING THE CONVERSATION TO SOOTHE OUR CHIMP

If our chimp has been triggered we will get into our response (fight, flight or freeze) mode and may get angry, frustrated, quiet or disengage. The head chatter taking place will get noisy and probably pretty unhelpful.

We all have head chatter going on. It might feel like a running commentary or a number of different thoughts having a conversation (or argument when the chimp is out). It will give voice to our thoughts, feelings, perceptions and evaluations and is like an inner coach – giving out instructions on what to do, how to do it and when to do it. It is really powerful and a great tool to use as an athlete.

Our head chatter can be really helpful. It can talk us into being more confident, can help us to focus and pay attention to the right things and, when we do it right, can reduce some of our anxiety. It can also be really unhelpful. When we are thinking negatively we can end up saying things to ourselves that we would never dream of saying to others. Our chatter is filtered through a malicious lens and we are nasty and vindictive, pulling apart our personality, choices and behaviours and situation without offering up any context or rationality like we offer to others. In the sporting environment that can destroy performance.

We can think of it a bit like food. You have a tough training session; you eat well beforehand, drink water during it, have some protein afterwards; you are nourishing your body to train hard and recover well. If you don't get a chance to eat beforehand, forget your water bottle and go straight to a fast-food place for food afterwards your improvement will suffer. The same goes on in your head. If you feed yourself good quality nutritious thoughts and words you will grow stronger and cope with the tougher times. If you ignore the hunger for feedback or, worse still, starve it of kind comments, it will become weak. So our head chatter feeds our brains, just as food feeds our bodies.

Where athletes have worked really hard to use helpful head chatter they can last longer in competition, quieten their chimp (to get into the challenge mindset), perform better, focus more, have higher confidence and perform their sporting skills to a higher level.

It does require work though. Simply trying to repress unhelpful thoughts doesn't work. In fact it is counterproductive as the more we try not to think about something the more you'll find it popping into your head. You need to feel in control and the content you use needs to be realistic and believable and regularly practised until it becomes a habit. Let's try two routes here to changing your conversation and soothing your chimp: thought stopping and reframing.

Thought stopping

Thought stopping isn't the supressing of unhelpful thoughts but the noticing of them and taking a purposeful decision to think about something more helpful. When we catch ourselves thinking unhelpfully in competition we have a word or an action we use to stop the thought and move on.

It is helpful to be really aware of the unhelpful thoughts you often have. You can build these up by doing the mindfulness and labelling activities in Chapter 2. These will be the type of thoughts that, if they are unhelpful and you have them in competition, you need to notice and shut down quickly.

<u>Question:</u> The action I will use to stop my unhelpful thought will be:

Say 'Stop' ☐

Say 'Not Now' ☐

Take a drink from my water bottle ☐

Ping a band on my wrist ☐

Pinch my hand   ☐

Snap my fingers   ☐

Squeeze my hand into a very tight fist and gradually release   ☐

Reframing

If we find we have similar unhelpful thoughts over and over again in competition we can learn to reframe those thoughts into much more helpful versions which help us perform better. Often the unhelpful thoughts are those which set off our chimp – fear of failure, judgement from others, losing to athletes we think we should beat, disappointing our parents – so finding a way to turn the fear into a facilitator helps our performance immensely.

We are not lying to ourselves, forcing in relentlessly positive phrases over the top of our true thoughts but trying to give a different, and more helpful, meaning to those thoughts. We need to practise it continually though so we are able to do it in the heat of the moment, such as when our chimp is likely to be triggered mid competition.

> Elite Insight: Charlie Spedding (running): What I was trying to develop wasn't positive thinking, it was specific thinking, like using the right words. I wanted to think in a precise way that would make me more successful.

When 24 runners took part in a study they were asked to do three 90-minute treadmill runs: one run with no specific instructions, one where they were asked to try to distract themselves and one where they were asked to reframe their thoughts. When they used reframing they felt they were able to run the same distance but said it felt like it needed less effort to do so and were able to cope better emotionally.

Ideally, we also use this process to remember our mastery over outcome focus. It gives us an easy theme to follow and keeps us focused on the moment so we are concentrating on the right things. For example, an original statement might be 'I can never do this skill'. It is unhelpful because it is negative and doesn't give us any instruction or action. If we reframed it to 'I'll master this skill if I keep practising like I am right now' it gives us a purpose to keep working and making an effort.

Activity: Reframe unhelpful head chatter

Our first job when we develop our reframing is to get those negative thoughts out of our head and onto the paper. Spend a couple of weeks filling in the left-hand column on the box below after training sessions or competitions with all the unhelpful thoughts you notice.

Then, when you have decent list, go through each, one by one, to think about how that thought could be reframed into something more helpful, motivating or process focused. Each reframed statement needs to be realistic and truthful. If you struggle to come up with something think about what you would say to a friend or teammate who was saying the same thing about themselves. How would you help them think about it differently?

Then get practising. It can feel really silly and awkward to start but once you get the hang of it you will have a brilliant tool in your toolkit forever more.

Some example reframes could be:

Negative/unhelpful thought	Could be reframed as
I'm out of my depth in this competition.	This competition is great preparation. I'll use it to learn as much as possible for the future.
There is too much wind to do this properly.	We are all having to deal with the wind. I will concentrate harder than everyone else.
I hate going up hills.	Hills make me stronger.
I can't do this.	I'm not great at this yet – but if I keep practising I will be.

Negative / unhelpful thought	Could be reframed as

SUCCESS STORY: SHAUN WRIGHT-PHILLIPS

Shaun Wright-Phillips played football over an 18-year professional career – for Manchester City, Chelsea and QPR in the UK and New York Red Bulls in the USA. He played in 36 matches for England and scored 6 goals for his country. He retired in 2019 aged 37.

> I had to learn to deal with pressure and expectation quite early. I got released from a club when I was 15 so it was something I had to come to terms with pretty quickly. I had to learn that there is always going to be downs and there is always going to be ups

and I had to work out a way for how I was going to deal with that so it doesn't affect my football. I realised it just comes down to opinions. Just because one coach or manager doesn't really like you at that specific time or you are not suited to that team or club, doesn't mean it is the same for everybody else so I just said 'OK, that is cool, that is what you think so I'll go and prove you wrong'. It helped me learn because even though there were things I was lacking I was more determined to make those things right to help with the pushback.

I didn't feel expectation from others as I didn't read the newspapers. I knew myself whether I played well or I played average or I played badly. Apart from the managers and your team-mates I didn't really listen to what other people had to say from the outside because it is just their view and what they think. For me the important people to listen to was your manager and your team mates – they are the only people who need to be able to say you didn't play well because they'll be able to give you an explanation. People that write stuff in the papers don't know what the manager said or what has been asked of you that game.

I have seen a load of people struggling in situations where sometimes the pressure is too much. I just enjoyed football that much that I never saw it as anything else. I never saw it as a job and I think that helped me. I just love the game. When I was growing up I took a football with me everywhere. Even if my mum asked me and my brother to go to the shop we wouldn't go to the shop without finding our football first.

I was very hard on myself whether it was a game or training if I did something sloppy. I knew what I expected from myself so I would get angry at myself but I learnt to just start from the beginning so I would say to myself 'for the next few passes just pass the ball simple and move'. Then as your confidence grows you can get back to what you really want to do. If I kept trying to do the hard stuff straight away I would just find that it never worked and I would have a bad game. I taught myself that I needed to go back and replay myself into the game.

No-one likes losing and sometimes no matter how well you play you still lose. When you haven't played too well and you lose then you just think about what you could have done different. A lot of what ifs come up. I realised I had to move on to the next game and do better. As soon as that game was played, that game was gone and now it was time to focus on the game coming up.

If I got nervous it was because I didn't want to let the people down who believed in me. As soon as the first whistle went and I got my first touch it would go though. I used to set myself targets and I found that helped me. I always went into games saying to myself these are my targets; in each half I have to try and get five or six crosses in and four shots.

In a game, no matter how red you see you are always under the ref's control and if you do anything that makes you see red then it is your team that suffer because they are a man less, so I always tried to put my team before my faults. If I missed a shot in games I'd say 'no problem – there is going to be another chance'.

If I did rage it would be for like 30 seconds but then you just have to get your head back in the game in case they try to take a free kick and you are out of position because you are too busy arguing. If I saw anyone on the opposing side seeing red and losing it then that helped me, because his concentration is not where it is meant to be. When he is frustrated he's going to do something rash which then either gets him a yellow or a red which benefits you, especially in my position as a winger.

CHAPTER **6**

I can concentrate

Concentrate. Focus. Pay attention. All words likely to have been yelled by our coaches at some point to try to get us to pay full awareness to what is going on in our event. For the purposes of performance these different words mean pretty much the same thing; keep your head in the game. And they have a point – a big point. It is really important that we do focus. We need our mental efforts to direct our physical efforts and we do that by focusing on the movements and actions which are most important at that time in a competition or match. Those who manage this, by paying attention to the right things at the right time, tend to be more successful.

> Elite Insight: Michael Phelps (swimming): When I'm focused there is not one single thing, person, anything that can stand in my way.

There are so many different calls on our attention before and during a competition. You can see some of them on this picture of a football match.

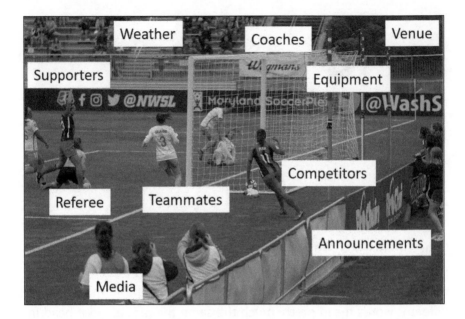

Some of these calls on our attention impact how we play. In football we need to know where the ball is at all times. In pole vault we need to feel the wind direction. In netball the whistle of the umpire is vital to listen out for. Some of the other calls on our attention are completely irrelevant – music being played in a rugby stadium, announcements for lost car keys in a hockey tournament, supporters yelling in a tennis match. They simply distract.

> Elite Insight: Rafael Nadal (tennis): What I battle hardest to do in a tennis match is to quiet the voices in my head to shut everything out of my mind but the contest itself and concentrate every atom of my being on the point I am playing.

When we get it right we are able to concentrate so we can apply deliberate mental effort on the things which are most important in our situation and let us shift that focus as and when we need to. It is like holding a torch, continually shining the light on the most helpful thing for us to notice in that moment. We need this shift to happen pretty effortlessly so we can continue to use our skills at the same time. Sport really is about being a master of multitasking. And this is really tricky as we aren't designed to do this so we are asking a lot of ourselves. But it is worth it. The better we can control where our attention goes, the better we perform.

When a study was run looking at the key elements of high performance, three of the eight elements they identified came from an athlete's ability to concentrate: being completely absorbed (often called flow), being relaxed even when concentrating and being super aware of their bodies and the environment.

Key question: In my sport what do I need to pay attention to?

Before we start the competition?

1.

2.

3.

Once the competition has started?

1.

2.

3.

At crunch moments?

1.

2.

3.

BECOMING BETTER AT CONCENTRATING

Concentration is a skill we can learn, but it is also something that develops with age. Experts suggest as you grow up you should be able to concentrate on a specific task for 2–3 minutes per year of your age. This means an 8-year old would be able to focus for around 20 minutes, a 12-year old for 30 minutes and a 16-year old for 40 minutes. If your match lasts 90 minutes with a half time, towards the end of each half you are likely to be getting pretty mentally fatigued and might need some strategies to be able to stay concentrating. If you are out on a golf course for up to 4 hours you will need to learn to switch your concentration on and off for just the moments you need it. If you are a sprinter then you have time to harness your attention well to focus on your immediate preparation and in your event.

Mental tapering

Concentrating requires mental effort and energy and when we get tired this is far less available. We will struggle to push our body when we are mentally fatigued. Long competitions do this but so does what we have been doing in the build-up. This means the first way to help us develop better concentration in our competitions is to be mentally fresh ahead of our events. Mental fatigue can have a big impact on how well we concentrate. Studies across a range of sports have found that athletes who were mentally tired (through doing really boring computer tests) ahead of a fitness challenge found the challenge harder and they hit exhaustion sooner.

Elite Insight: Jonny Wilkinson (rugby): I realised that we tire mentally too and when it happens to me the enjoyment drains from whatever it is I am doing.

Mental fatigue can come when we have been studying hard, trying to do difficult things or handling events like exams, coursework, house moves, projects or difficult family issues. Being stressed can also impact. It is the effort we have to put into coping with the stress that makes us mentally fatigued. Think about the stressors you have to deal with before a competition and consider how you deal with them. Do they ever make you feel mentally tired?

Ideally, we would avoid all stressful or mentally tiring activities before a competition. Life is not that simple though. Especially if you do a summer sport when competitions coincide with exams. There are a few things you can do to help though.

- If you have an important competition making some time in the few days beforehand to properly relax will be helpful; movie watching, music listening or chatting with friends are all good to keep you mentally fresh.
- If you are physically doing less exercise right before your competition so you feel fresher when you need to perform, try not to fill the time with extra projects, schoolwork or revision.
- If you have any control of your study schedule then use the time before a competition to focus on basic admin tasks rather than one which needs lots of attention and effort.

- Where you can, organise competition packing, transport and details on how you will get there a few days before your competition so you don't end up doing it last minute (and becoming really stressed).

- If you have no choice but to do lots of mentally fatiguing tasks in the week before a really big competition try to get extra sleep to help you recover.

- In long competitions perhaps try to switch your focus on and off so it is there when you need it.

Fixing our spotlight

When we are competing we have to continually filter information coming at us so we can block out the things which will distract and focus on the things which we need to be aware of. This process is tiring and slow. A faster process is to choose how we want to concentrate ahead of competition and let our spotlight follow that strategy.

What our spotlight needs to focus on will depend on our sport and the position we hold (if in a team). You can ask yourself in training or practice 'where is my focus right now'. If it is giving us too much information it will be hard to filter and make a good decision. If it is in the wrong direction then you'll get distracted. If you focus too much on one thing you may miss something really important.

When we are calm and in a challenge mindset we can switch focus pretty easily and know we are using what is right for the moment. If we get into a threat mindset (with our chimp coming out to cause chaos) it is much harder. We already know that the threat mindset increases our heart rate, makes our breathing quicker and makes our muscles tighter but it also really narrows our focus so we are only able to concentrate on small things ahead of us rather than all the things we want and might need to.

Activity: Coach on a shoulder

In Chapter 5 we talked about using head chatter to help us handle the stress of competition but we can also use it to direct our attention effectively. We do this by giving ourselves specific instructions, just like you have a (tiny little) coach sitting on your shoulder.

The phrase you say should be short and sharp. Something you can repeat rhythmically to keep your attention in the right place. If you worry you might forget it you can write it on your hand or your water bottle so you get a regular reminder. It works particularly well when you use the phrase you pick to work on your strength, accuracy or fine motor skills. Sometimes it is just one word which helps you focus on something very specific. It clicks you to attention. It may cover a behaviour you need to use to be successful.

> Elite Insight: Kelly Smith (football). "I remember saying to myself, 'Put the ball down in a good spot. Focus on the frame of the goal. Keep your head over the ball. And don't put it over the bar.' I kept repeating that over and over again in my head."

Most important, just like Kelly Smith, is to give yourself positive instructions, where you tell yourself what to do, not what to avoid. 'Focus on the ball' is much more effective than 'don't look at the stands'. When we tell ourselves not to do things our brain likes to put that thing slap bang in the middle of our head so we end up focusing on it.

Here you can practise a couple of instructions you could give yourself for different situations mid competition.

Situation	Purpose of instruction	Instruction

Sometimes, in dull practice sessions or if you are doing endurance sports where you will be competing for hours you might want to try to distract yourself from the boredom or discomfort you are feeling. It can be a really good strategy to give your mind a break from working hard. But, this strategy is rubbish when you have tonnes going on and you need to stay on top of it. Daydreaming about lunch is a good way to get through some tough hill repeats but might see you de-selected if you try it in sprint drills which require much more concentration.

In these moments where we need to concentrate we need to be really proactive with what we focus on. A really popular action is body checking. In endurance-based sports you would mentally skim up and down your body to adjust pace, strategy or technique. In ball-based sports you would reflect where you are compared to the ball and to other people, and in all other sports you can focus on how your body is feeling and what it should be doing. It helps you become hyper aware of your body's actions and functions – heart rate, muscle tension, breathing rate – so you can adapt and focus on the right things.

Activity: Mind over muscle

Go back to the questions you answered at the beginning of this chapter on what you need to pay attention to once the competition has started.

Then think about each element you wrote down and pick a part of your body you can focus on to help you do that better.

Things requiring attention once competition has started	What I will focus on

An example for a 5,000-metre runner would be:

Things requiring attention once competition has started	What I will focus on
Keeping an eye on my foot strike and stride pattern	My feet – counting my steps for a minute once I go past each km marker
Keeping my arms swinging forward (rather than side to side)	Repeating 'drive forward' with my arms when I catch myself swinging them
Breathing consistently until the final 500 m	Being at a pace where I could just about speak if I had to

TYPES OF ATTENTION

There are lots of things we know we need to concentrate on in a competition. Where it gets tricky is when they keep changing and we need to keep switching our focus. There are four types of attention and we need to pick the right one at the right time.

The four types are based on two scales: width and direction. The width scale sees us needing to sometimes go narrow (focused on a specific thing) through to very wide (the whole environment). The direction scale covers our internal thoughts through to external cues from others. How do we know which one to use when?

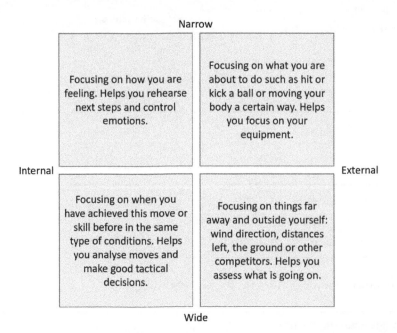

Narrow

Focusing on how you are feeling. Helps you rehearse next steps and control emotions.	Focusing on what you are about to do such as hit or kick a ball or moving your body a certain way. Helps you focus on your equipment.
Focusing on when you have achieved this move or skill before in the same type of conditions. Helps you analyse moves and make good tactical decisions.	Focusing on things far away and outside yourself: wind direction, distances left, the ground or other competitors. Helps you assess what is going on.

Internal   External

Wide

When we put our attention in the wrong 'zone' we'll start to notice things which are really unhelpful for our performance. Let's take our 5,000-metre runner for example.

On the start line they want a narrow-internal focus, staying calm and thinking about their strategy. If they had a wide-external focus they would be looking along the line spotting who looks fit and fast and might beat them. Towards the end of the race they will want a wide-internal focus to make the best tactical decision. Having a narrow-external would be ok (focusing on how to pick feet up and chase others down the track) but a narrow-internal focus would be disastrous as that might involve thinking about how much discomfort they were in.

Not being able to get into a challenge mindset before a competition can have risky implications for our ability to concentrate once our event starts. Our level of activation and how anxious we are can impact how well our brains process information, and that means we may well end up focusing on irrelevant things.

Even though we should be able to switch quickly between attention types most of us have a style we prefer and feel most comfortable with.

Question: What is your attentional style?

Internal (focused on own thoughts and behaviours) ☐

Or

External (hyper aware of what others are doing) ☐

And

Narrow (don't tend to get distracted – but might not
    see big picture) ☐

Or

Wide (well aware of everything going on may miss
    what is right in front of you) ☐

When you know your style you can figure out how to use it well in competition so you can use the positive parts of it to perform at your best.

SWITCHING ATTENTION

If we continually miss the right cues in a competition we are likely to perform badly. We need to be incredibly speedy at decision-making and following the right cues is part of that. If we take football for example, it is estimated that each player has to make between 8 and 10 tactical decisions every minute. In a full match that is 720 decisions. The fewer cues being noticed the fewer high-quality decisions and the lower the performance given. So, it is not just understanding how we direct our attention (internal or external), how deep it goes (wide or narrow) but also how quickly we can shift that focus.

When relaxed we are likely to be using a wide attentional style so we are looking around, quite chilled, scanning for all sorts of information. When we are in a threat mindset our focus becomes super narrow and internal – just concentrating on tiny things or thoughts in our own head. They might be important but so will be other things that we are completely missing.

If we think about basketball. Ideally a player will have a wide attentional style when in the middle of the court to spot teammates to throw to and opposition to dodge. But when that same player is right by the hoop and has the ball in their hands they immediately need to narrow their focus, blocking out the noise and distraction and focusing purely on where they want the ball to go. It is really important that we can manipulate our focus so we can use the attentional style that matches how we need to perform right then.

Activity: Focus shifting

To practise shifting your focus you need to get onto YouTube. Search for videos of your sport. Pick an athlete who plays a similar position to you or has a likeminded approach to you and put a cross next to each type of attentional style you spot that they should be using. Try to watch 5 minutes of the video.

Narrow-external	☐	☐	☐	☐	☐	☐	☐	☐	☐	☐
Wide-external	☐	☐	☐	☐	☐	☐	☐	☐	☐	☐
Wide-internal	☐	☐	☐	☐	☐	☐	☐	☐	☐	☐
Narrow-internal	☐	☐	☐	☐	☐	☐	☐	☐	☐	☐

Count up afterwards how many in each type to spot and divide by 300 (overall seconds you watched) and you'll get an idea from your sport how often in seconds (i.e. every 20 seconds) you should be able to switch attention.

DEALING WITH DISTRACTIONS

When we have figured out attention we then have to deal with distractions. Distractions can really stop us from being able to concentrate and make it impossible to focus on what is important – massively harming our performance.

There are three types of distraction: internal, external and outcome. Internal distractions will cover our own worries or anxiety, the unhelpful head chatter we have, feeling tired or poorly, our tummy rumbling because we are hungry. External distractions cover the environment around us. They can be visual (like crowds, other competitors or scoreboards, camera flashes or our parents yelling advice or support), auditory (supporters chanting, phones going off or music over the Tannoy) or multi-sensory such as the rain hammering it down or gusts of strong wind. If you are in a sport like archery, shooting or fencing these external distractions can have a big impact on how precise you are able to be in your movements. Outcome-based distractions pull us into thinking about past or the future and wondering what will happen if we win or lose. As we covered in Chapter 1, successful athletes are able to spend more time 'in the moment' focused on mastering and displaying their skills, rather than trying to win, or worse, trying not to lose. They focus on 'how' to perform well rather than the 'outcome' of performing well.

Some distractions are doubly distracting because they trigger your chimp (Chapter 5) and put you into a threat mindset so you go into a narrow-internal frame and can't switch into the frame you actually need to be in at that moment.

If you start to notice any of these internal-, external- or outcome-type distractions your attentional focus will shift. Often to entirely the wrong dimension. Then you need to spend even more mental energy getting it back to where it is helpful, making you extra fatigued. And when we are fatigued we can't concentrate so well. It is an annoying vicious circle. To break the circle we either need to reduce as many distractions as possible or practise doing our sport with them all going on around us so we get used to them.

Activity: Distraction mapping

Circle all the distractions you notice when you go to competitions:

Outcome

Shame
Lose
Win
Qualify
Prize money
Name in paper
Sports board at school
Beat our rivals
Move up the league

Internal

Embarrassment
Emotions
Thirst
Worry
Boredom
Anxiety
Random thoughts
Soreness
Tiredness
Niggles or pain

External

Photo flashes
Bright sunshine
Scoreboards
Crowd noise
Sledging
Public announcements
Windy
Rain

A distraction may be something pretty small – music too loud, supporters booing, umpire giving unfair judgments – but under pressure minor irritations can quickly become major frustrations and turn into a 'hot button' of anger. When one of these distractions becomes a hot button it triggers our chimp. We then need to get our chimp calm as quick as possible, before it has had much chance to cause chaos. As well as bananas, chimps tend to feed off uncertainty. Uncertainty can come when we are missing boundaries and structures. To begin to reel them back in we can set up some routines. These help us stop, reset and get our human back in change. Just as we set a pre-performance routine in Chapter 2 to get in control of our threat mindset before competition, in competition we can use a mid-competition routine to reset after our hot button has been pushed.

Activity: Hot button reset

Your hot button reset needs to be very short, entirely driven by your sport and what you get time or space for. Focuses on helping you get back to your optimal level of activation.

We try to follow the four R's:

- Respond – think about what your face and body do when your chimp gets triggered. If you give away your thoughts in your face you are giving lots of power to your competitor. Practise masking those faces of frustration or annoyance.

- React – a positive personal response such as walking to the edge of a court or pitch, snapping a band on your wrist or pinching your hand. Something immediate to snap you out of the anger.

- Relax – something to calm you – usually some deep breathing to reduce your activation level and get you back into a challenge mindset.

- Refocus – getting out head back into the competition and remembering: What do I need to do to perform well?

Hot Button:	
	What I will do
Respond	
React	
Relax	
Refocus	

Let's use an example from a golfer:

Hot Button: Just hit a poor shot that I would usually nail. I can feel myself getting angry and annoyed.	
	What I will do
Respond	Shoulders down, smile, face relaxed Redo the swing as I would have preferred it to have gone
React	Taking a sip of water and put a sweet in my mouth. Notice the taste of the sweet
Relax	While walking to ball do three rounds of colourful breathing to slow down heart rate
Refocus	Repeat my refocus phrase: 'Patience and process'

SUCCESS STORY: REBECCA ADLINGTON

Rebecca Adlington OBE fell in love with swimming at the age of 3 and spent 21 years in the sport, retiring once she had earnt multiple Olympic, World, Commonwealth and European medals. She competed in the Beijing and London Olympic games bringing home two gold and two bronze medals in the 400 and 800 metres. As well as all those medals she has the ultimate accolade; she actually has a swim centre named after her. She now runs programmes helping children learn to love swimming as much as she does. Here she tells us how she kept her concentration and focus in training and racing.

Before my races started my coach would give me three things to focus on. He said if you think about more than three things you just lose your way, it is just too much. And he was right. It confuses me and I get more stressed. My three things were always technical stuff to do with stroke rate and stroke length and I just used to repeat them and that for me was how I would stay focused and in the zone.

I never listened to music because I found with music I would zone out and switch off and I can't concentrate. For me music is a way to switch off and I had to stay really focused so music was a distraction to me.

If I paid attention to everyone else I would lose my thoughts so I used visualisation. Visualising me diving in the water, me swimming the race. Visualisation was really helpful because then when I then swam it, it felt a bit Deja vu. 'Oh I've done this before'. It wasn't something unknown. I found that really helpful to me to just stay in that zone and I found it helped with my nerves as well. My sport psychologist helped me make it a bit more focused and he helped me visualise the journey and the process. He fine-tuned it so I was visualising the right things. I wanted to concentrate on swimming my race and swimming the way I want to instead of getting worked up about others so when I stood behind the block I would visualise drawing a pair of curtains until all I could see was my lane. It really focused me and it stopped me focusing on everybody else so I could just swim my own race.

You can't concentrate in all races, all the time. I don't think it is physically possible to keep doing it every single time. Obviously the more important competitions you did but I can't say I concentrated for over 8 minutes on every single 800 I did. Sometimes I used to lose count. Sometimes I used to think about what I was going to have for my lunch. Sometimes a song would pop in my head. But at a major final or competition it was a lot more important to concentrate and to stay focused and I always used to come back to those same three things. Something I had to work on was not to focus on the pain. A lot of my efforts were trying to take the concentration away from the pain and keep the concentration focused on the tactics and the race.

Emotional and mental fatigue would really get to me so I would have to take myself away from situations. Especially at the Olympics because, firstly you are a sports fan so get emotionally involved in every single race and secondly these are my team mates and people I care about and if they don't swim well I get upset and if they do swim well I get elated and cheering so my emotions are going all over the place. It used to take a toll on me and I just wasn't as focused and I couldn't concentrate, I was a bit all over the place. It just drained me.

You can't isolate yourself all of the time though so you will have to deal with distractions. And you do need the familiarity. I like to know the routes that I had to be taking; so how long does it take me to get from the warmup pool. Where is my nearest changing room to get ready? A lot of the time I think the distractions come from who you surround yourself with. I naturally gravitated to a lot of people in the team who were very calming. My coach always made an effort to be very calm around me and I found that very helpful. And others like my sport psychologist on the team and my family. It really calmed me to see my family. You need to do whatever works for you in the competition environment.

CHAPTER 7

I can bounce back

Getting left on the bench or not making the first team, moving up age groups or from school to college teams, having your coach move on, having to move coaching set-ups yourself, injury or illness, having to stop playing for a while, starting new relationships, not being able to afford to play your sport or having to dedicate more time to school or a job; however good, focused and dedicated you are, these are all things which could happen to you as an athlete. Setbacks happen to everyone. And they are annoying and frustrating and difficult.

If the setback is an injury it especially sucks. Injuries can cause pain, stop us training and competing, make us feel mentally rubbish and see us continually worry about getting another injury. But they are usually not as bad as we initially fear.

Setbacks involving injuries are really common. A study of the Great Britain 2014 Winter Olympic Team showed that in the 18 days of the event 39% of the 56-member team experienced some kind of injury. Winter Sport competitions are clearly going to have a high injury risk but even day-to-day sport sees a risk of injury. Over 2% of A&E attendances per year are due to sports injuries (nearly 400,000 visits) and these are the most serious acute issues that come from a fall or crash or clash. Where injuries are chronic (long term and developing from a niggle) they will never make it to A&E but will need medical support and may require months off sport recovering.

The process goals focus we developed earlier in this book should help you cope better with any setbacks as you will be used to focusing on improvement rather than outcomes. You should also have been realistic in your approaches to your outcome goals so will have anticipated that disruptions might have come along. Expectations of some type of setback can reduce the feeling of unfairness that often comes with them.

If your setback is an injury it is really tough because as well as the frustration and grief for the events you are missing you might be in pain and have to stop training. You might feel lots of different emotions such as devastation, feeling cheated, restlessness or isolation. And even when recovered some athletes develop a fear of re-injury which holds you back from being brave in your sport.

It is not unusual to struggle with poor mental health when injuries or setbacks occur. Many of us love our sports because they help us deal with pressures or stresses. This is backed up by studies showing that playing sport can be as effective at dealing with feelings of depression as medication is. But if you can't do your sport for a while you don't just feel rubbish for missing out but you also miss out on the opportunity to physically release the pent-up frustration or have any head space to calm down and put things into perspective.

We all tend to experience our own injuries differently. You may have similar physical factors to someone else but you will respond to it mentally based on your social circle, personality traits and previous experiences so you will end up dealing with it very differently.

GROWING FROM SETBACKS

Setbacks, while really annoying at the time, can actually be a really good way to learn and develop strengths that we didn't realise we had. Whether it is a set of really poor results, injury, being dropped from a team or watching others progress faster than you, these setbacks can be a vital part of your sporting development. They can give you new perspectives, help you find better ways of working and boost your motivation. If you do the right things during your setback you can come back a stronger, more focused athlete.

Lauren Steadman is a Paratriathlete and brings this growth through setback approach to life. In the Rio Paralympics Steadman went 25 metres in the wrong direction during the swim. She had to swim 25 metres back to get back on track which meant her race plan of getting ahead and staying ahead fell apart. After the bike and the run she crossed the finish line in second place. Afterwards she said "I remember crossing the line with a sense of relief but a massive sense of disappointment. Angry at myself. I took seven months out after that. I was so angry. I felt I hadn't done myself justice. I worked hard, came back with a new sense of energy and excitement. I was over the moon. Went to World Champs and got a Gold medal."

What we learn is dependent on the type of setback, the help we get and our response to it. If it comes because of some body weaknesses then it may force us to incorporate more strength and conditioning work into our sports practice which then makes us stronger. If we have had great advice when dealing with our setback, it may mean we learn some better coping skills which will help us deal better with stress in future. Setbacks can open up opportunities to engage with more experts in our sport and learn from them. They are also pretty good ways to get some perspective on our sport and help us see what we love about it, or dislike so we can adapt it better to our lives once we get going again.

Elite Insights: Catherine Spencer (rugby): Sometimes following a physical injury, athletes will come back stronger; they have been broken in some way and need to rehabilitate effectively to get back to fitness, but this is often accompanied by a strong resolve and an increased motivation. ... I experienced a stronger resolve and motivation to play for England after my injury.

The growth we can get can come from reframing our setback as a learning opportunity. You can do this through setback analysis where you are able to see what is and isn't working well so you can make changes where you need to.

Activity: Setback analysis

Your goal when doing this is to be as unemotional as possible. Setbacks and injuries are really frustrating but to do this well you need to put the frustration to one side. Perhaps try to see your situation as a friend would so you can be kinder to yourself and less emotive.

What do you think caused the setback:

Which elements of the setback I could control:

Which elements of the setback I could not control:

Were there any of the uncontrollable elements I could have influenced:

Action plan: What I could do differently in future so it doesn't happen again:

Example: Here is an example from a cross-country runner who tripped on a tree root and twisted their ankle so you can see how a finished setback analysis might look like.

What caused the setback: Tripping over a tree root.

Elements I could control:

1. Whether I looked down at the ground in that moment
2. How high I lift my feet when I run
3. Where I position myself against the other runners

Elements I could not control:

1. That the tree root was there
2. The other runners around me shoving their way through
3. The wet weather which made it really muddy and slippery

Any of the uncontrollable elements I could have influenced:

1. I could have checked out the course beforehand and spotted where the risky areas were and made a plan for them.
2. I could have worn different spikes in my shoes to give me more grip in the mud.

Action plan:

Always check out the course earlier in the day before a cross-country race.

Ask those in races before mine if there is anything I need to look out for.

Take all my spikes with me to races.

COPING WITH SETBACKS

Feeling angry, frustrated, scared, lonely, anxious or fragile are all perfectly valid responses to a setback. How you specifically respond to an injury can be impacted by up to 55 different factors. These might include your attitudes towards change, the coping strategies you regularly use, whether you identify as an athlete or someone who just does sport and your different personality traits. The athletes who tend to suffer most with injuries or setbacks are those who don't have much support around them, mainly focus on outcomes, are generally pessimistic, have low confidence and are more introverted.

> Elite Insight: Jonny Wilkinson (rugby): Dealing with each stumbling block had not come easy to me. Tears of frustration, upset and too much self-pity punctuated the journey. I was stronger for it in so many different ways than I could ever have considered before. I was not just a better player but an all more balanced all round person.

The ideal response is called 'problem-focused coping' where we try to minimise the source of the stress by finding out lots about the problem so we can do something about it. If we become preoccupied with the emotional impact of the setback (such as feeling anxious) and we try to distract ourselves to avoid thinking about it we do not cope as well or recover as quickly.

Here we can see in an interview with the BBC that Andy Murray made changes when he returned from an injury. He used problem-focused coping to make sure his body stays strong. "My post-match routine has changed a little bit – I'm making sure I get all my recovery stuff done first as I have to take care of my body first and foremost. I was straight into the ice bath after the match for about 12 minutes and then had a shower, did some stretching and had a massage with my physio. Then I had some food, completed my media commitments and then I went back and did another 20-30 minutes with my physio before heading home. Previously, I would probably have done the one session with my physio and that's it but I need to do a little bit more now to look after my body."

If, like Murray, you use the time out from training and competition as an opportunity to understand why you got injured it will help you reflect better on all your sport. Maybe you have been too focused on your sport in the past and might want to consider other hobbies too. Or if you haven't focused hard enough in the past, the time away might reignite your motivation and make you want to get back to it. A setback, approached with the right mindset, can sometimes be the kick up the bum we need to make changes.

It is also important to find ways to protect ourselves after a setback. One of the really tough things can be being sidelined from sport and feeling like everyone else is out there still playing and progressing much faster. We don't want to be left behind and we don't want to lose all we have worked for. One way this feels unavoidable is through social media.

Social media is brilliant for athletes. It can be a good way to show you are worthy of sponsorship, to read great articles to help you improve in your sport and to stay in touch with your teammates and competitors. But if you are not able to compete or train right now it can really suck to have other's excitement and successes waved in our face. Apps that track our training or performances can also be helpful in regular times when you can see what speed you were running at or how good your heart rate variability is right now but all they do when you are off injured is highlight how much fitness you are losing. So we need a tech strategy which protects our mental health while we deal with setbacks.

Activity: Plan your tech strategy

Ask yourself:

How do I benefit from social media?

What risks do I have from social media?

Which channels help me and which ones make me feel bad?

Which apps which track my health or sport do I use?

How does each of these help me?

Are there any apps or specific people on social media where I feel worse after seeing them?

From these answers work out what you will look at and which ones you might delete off your phone until you are back on your feet.

GETTING BACK IN CONTROL

Our response to injuries impacts how well and how fast we recover and whether we grow from the injury. As it is really likely we will get injured at some point it is vital we have other things we love in our life so we don't feel like we have lost everything. We can learn strategies to help us do this and one of these is a six-step approach: anger, information gathering, finding experts, goal setting, filling the space and social support.

Activity: Six-step setback approach

Step 1: Anger. It is perfectly ok to be angry about what you have lost. You are grieving for the season you thought you were going to have. But try to cut the sulking and anger down to 2 days max. Then it is time to get focused on your comeback.

Step 2: Get knowledgeable. You can only make decisions based on the information in front of you. So you need to find that information. Ask your coach, teammates or friends if they have suffered anything similar and where they got information and support from. This process of finding out more about your setback is called instrumental coping, and studies have found it helps you deal better with the setback and recover quicker. You can also try to figure out why the setback happened. If it is due to a fall, clash or sudden impact, how can you reduce your risk of it happening again. If it is a chronic injury it may have been something rumbling away over a long period and might need some time with your coach or a physiologist to work out what caused it. If it is an illness or other type of setback then maybe a chat with a parent or caregiver could help you figure out what caused the issue. Once you are better informed you can put in place changes and set up a system to get you recovered.

Step 3: Finding experts to help. Once we know what is likely to be wrong we need to find people to help us fix it. If it is an injury you may need a physio, osteopath, sports massage therapist, specialist sports doctor or GP. If it is another type of setback, you may need friends, family or a teacher. Most important, you need someone you trust and respect so you feel comfortable in following their advice.

Elite Insight: Dame Kelly Holmes (track): In my athletics career, my injuries have caused frequent and frustrating setbacks and tears but I have always picked myself up thanks to the help and support of the fantastic people I have been lucky enough to have round me.

Step 4: Goal-set your comeback. Researchers have found that those who recover the best are those who are as serious about their recovery as they are about their training. Setting specific goals to help you get back to full mental and physical fitness. When researchers looked at studies covering almost 1,000 injured athletes they found those who focused on things like goal setting returned to sport quicker and got back to similar levels of fitness and skill as they were before the injury. The goals need to be really process driven though to make following them easy and for you to see regular progress, and feel good about making that progress.

Step 5: Filling the gap. When you are off sport you'll have time to fill. If injured you might have some rehab exercises to fill the space and you can use the spare time to catch up on schoolwork but you do need to find something fun to fill the extra time. You could find new fun things to do (such as a new hobby or catching up on movies you've missed), catch up on schoolwork so you are ahead and have more time when you get back to your sport or learn new mental skills which will help you when you get back up to full fitness. Learning mental skills for your sport (as you are doing in this book) is particularly helpful as studies have shown that athletes who use them are less likely to get injured, by up to 50% fewer injuries in some sports who use techniques like imagery.

Step 6: Stay social. When you are out of sport it can turn your world upside down so it is really important you don't lose all of it. The social interaction you can get with your friends is actually seen as a really valuable buffer, reducing the negative emotions you feel. Studies have found the more social support you have the fewer depressive symptoms you are likely to get in response to a setback. Think about who you might go to for emotional, technical, informational and motivational support. And while you may not be able to physically join in, you can still go to training. In fact, those who stay in touch with their club and remain in touch with team-mates recover quicker. You could also benefit by helping out at your club – perhaps by mentoring or teaching younger athletes as it keeps your skills and knowledge up to date and helps give you a sense of purpose.

REDUCING FUTURE RISK

It is important we get back in control of more than just our setback. If we want to stay in our sport for a long time we need to get in control of our risk factors for injury.

There are psychological factors which can increase our risk of injury. We might expect these to be physical ones (such as over training) or environmental (so tripping over the outside of the court) but there are also risks based upon the culture and attitudes in your sport (such as gymnastics where some gymnasts have previously been pushed by coaches to become unhealthily underweight or team cultures suggesting that you need pain to improve).

Elite Insight: Richard Kruse (fencing): It is very important to stay injury free. The dangerous injuries are the ones which come about because of doing the wrong technique. Sprinters spend more time keeping injury free than they do sprinting and by the end of my career that was true for me too. I would spend more time doing my warmup, my core session and my stretch off at the end, than I actually spent fencing.

Some risk factors are very personal to us. They might be based on our age, how strong or flexible we are, if we have had previous injuries and some of our personality traits. There are other factors though which are outside of us, much more around our sport, the rules, the amount of contact, accepted cultures and behaviours, typical weather conditions and the amount of equipment involved.

One reason stress can increase our risk of injury is that thinking about the issue causing us stress can distract us from training properly and safely. If your head is full of worries about the way you have been treated by friends or whether you will pass your exams, you are less likely to pay attention to vital cues around you and so more likely to fall over, to use poor technique or to lose concentration at a crucial moment.

Another reason stress can cause us injury is that stress can lead to our peripheral vision becoming narrowed so we may miss important things going on. Often this means we simply play worse but if we are in a contact sport we may well not notice a tackle coming our way so we don't have time to safely prepare for it. Stress also leads to physical responses in our bodies, one of which is muscle tension. When our muscles get tight during training or competition our flexibility, co-ordination and movement patterns reduce so we are more likely to get injured. In studies where coaches helped athletes manage their stress levels, injury levels also reduced.

A further way to reduce the risk of future injury is to really get to know your body. When you know what feels 'normal' to you then you can spot when something has got out of sync and work on fixing it. One way we can do this is through a technique called 'progressive muscle relaxation' (PMR). It doesn't just help you learn your body but also teaches it to relax and minimise your anxiety levels – something else that should reduce your risk of injury.

Activity: Progressive muscle relaxation

PMR is where you tense and relax muscles in one muscle group at a time so you can learn to appreciate the differences in sensation between very tense and totally relaxed muscles. You would use this technique at home (and it needs lots of practice) so you can begin to detect tension in your muscles and so you can switch off some of the activation which comes about ahead of competitions.

You need somewhere quiet with something to lie or sit on where you won't be disrupted. It can take up to about half an hour when you first learn this, but you'll soon get much faster.

1. Get into position and close your eyes.
2. Start by taking five slow, deep breaths.
3. Next, focus your attention on your feet. Do one foot at a time. And clench one really, really hard.
4. Notice the tension in the muscles of your foot. Count slowly to 10. Decrease the tension to about halfway. Count slowly to 10 again and then release the tension completely. Repeat and this time really notice how the muscles feel.
5. Keep your foot relaxed for around 15 seconds and then move onto the other foot.
6. Work your way up your body with each set of muscles until you reach your head. Your forehand should be the last section you relax.
7. When you have done your whole body, take a few deep breaths, slowly shake out your legs and arms and move your head from side to side and slowly stand up.

Questions to ask yourself as you do your muscle relaxation:

*   Do my muscles feel warm, heavy, tight or loose?
*   Do my muscles feel different when tense and relaxed? Specifically, try to notice the difference between the zero, minimum, medium and maximum levels of tension.

If you would prefer to listen to someone talking you through the process then google: 'progressive muscle relaxation audio' and lots of great audio clips can be downloaded.

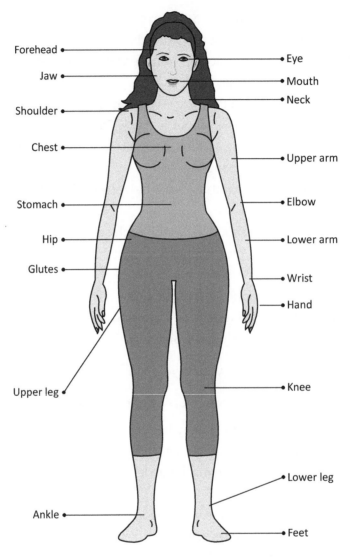

Here on this female athlete's picture are all the areas to focus on in your PMR.

SUCCESS STORY: JOE WEATHERLEY

Joe Weatherley is a batsman for Hampshire. He started playing club cricket at the age of 8 and captained the England under-19 team. At 23 he has just faced his first major setback in his sporting career.

> I broke my ankle last June. I was playing football in the warm-up. It was my first injury so it was definitely a new challenge. I did all the rehab last summer and into the winter and went through pre-season in the new year and then COVID hit and so I haven't played a game for Hampshire for about 12 months. It is strange – I'm 23 and it feels like a big part of my learning and career that has been impacted.
>
> As it was my first injury I found I went through phases of: 'why me?' and anger and frustration and 'am I gonna lose my spot in the team?' I was getting jealous of the guys still playing and maybe taking my spot. But then I got my teeth stuck into the rehab and I enjoyed that because it felt like every day I am getting closer to getting back on the park and that progression. Equally it was quite dark, when you are at the training ground but you don't see your team mates because you are in the gym, that is quite difficult.
>
> There are stages when you realise this is fine and I'm actually quite grateful to have a break but yes I'd rather be playing and getting better but actually this is my first injury and I'm going to use it as an opportunity to find new hobbies and develop myself and find things away from the game and take a bit of a breather. The time out gave me a chance to get back into my degree and I got to spend more time with my mates. We give up so many social opportunities as sportsmen so I actively went out and saw some mates I wouldn't normally see. The time out helped re-establish what was important; I spent a lot of time with family and friends.

After a while I then went through the process of 'how can I get better?' I went to the coaches and said: What do I do well? What can I get better at? Where do you see me? I asked all those kind of questions to a whole different bunch of coaches. It helped me get over the initial anger, frustration phase and those conversations helped me to re-engage with everything.

In some ways having an injury is a really negative thing but I was really determined to turn it into a positive. I feel the injury has made me a better cricketer and person just because having the injury can make you realise how much you enjoy it and appreciate things. It didn't feel like it at the time but looking back, I think it provided more learning opportunities than if I hadn't had it before.

With Hampshire we have such great support. We have two sport psychologists, a personal development and welfare officer, family, friends, management, team-mates and doctors and they couldn't have been better in many ways. It was nice to have other team-mates, who had gone through actually worse injuries than I had, to speak to them to get their view. Equally there was a support network of management who were really actively checking in and actually not saying a whole lot but just offering 'I'm here if you need me and lets grab a coffee just to chat'. It might not be cricket related but it actually went a long way.

I found I needed progression to know next week this is what we will aim for. The science and medicine team set out a plan with little objective markers about how I was recovering and what I needed to hit to progress to the next thing and that was always the focus on getting better.

While I was off I listened to a lot of the match coverage and it probably wasn't healthy. I would go through periods where I was like I don't want to listen or watch this but I can't not watch it because I felt so attached to it. It is my team. In some ways you want to be as far away from it as you can and in other ways you want to be living and breathing it like you are in it.

When I get back into matches I know the headspace I operate best in and that is a relaxed headspace. I try and breathe and relax and focus on loosening my arms and dropping my shoulders. When I am stressed my shoulders are high and I know if I relax them they drop and everything lifts and that helps me relax and I am chilled and I can then just let all the hours of practice that I have done come out and help me perform.

CHAPTER 8

I can belong

Sport should always add something extra to your life, not detract from it, nor become everything in it. Dedication, passion and focus are brilliant – they can help make you an excellent athlete. But they can also make you a lonely athlete if you give up everything else for your sport. When we feel lonely we might also resent our sport as it feels like we are sacrificing everything else for it. However, if we look at what we do with our sport as 'investing' then we are putting our efforts, time and energy into something we love. It is hard to get the balance right but when we do get it right we not only achieve success but also have people to share that success with.

It is easiest to get this balance right when we have two things in place: a sense of our own identity and to be in a place and environment where we know people have our back and are on our side. We'll explore both in this chapter.

WHO AM I?

As a teenager you are working out who you are. You get to break free of the pressures and perceptions that have been imposed by parents and teachers and start to understand what you love, what you care about, what you want to do with your own life. Where your sport fits into that is important as you may well have begun it because your family or friends did that sport but if you want to stay motivated and put in the work you need to make it your own choice. This is probably the hardest part of being a teenager – having to really work out who you are and what matters to you – and it is completely normal to struggle with this.

If you feel you are an athlete above all else then that will shape how you behave and act and what else you let come into your life. It will often be helpful to your results as it gives you motivation to train, helps you work consistently, means you prepare well for competition and helps you make good choices (such as eating well or getting enough sleep).

This 'one track mind' might give you options but it can also take some away. It makes a very public statement about what you believe is important. To someone who might employ you in the future it might say you are dedicated and loyal and work hard. To a future boyfriend or girlfriend it might say you won't have much time to spend with them.

Your external identity might also be placed upon you. If you perform well, have lots of success and are talked about in your sport others might link you really closely with that sport, becoming known at school as Tennis Girl or Hockey Boy. If you love your sport you probably won't mind but if you don't or you are going through a tough time with your sport and feel you are being overtaken or you are injured, then it can make you feel really miserable and like no one else sees all the other things you have going for you. In fact, research across those retiring in football, rugby and cricket found that the loss of identity when they stopped playing contributed to over half of them struggling with their mental health.

Elite Insight: Catherine Spencer (rugby): I felt I had no personal identity. After twenty years of looking up, aiming to get to the next stage in my rugby career, for the first time I found myself constantly looking back. Looking back at what I had been, looking back at what we could have achieved if things had been different.

So, how much of your time and energy and efforts your sport takes up is important. How much do you feel like an athlete? What else do you feel like? A student, musician, friend, son or daughter, brother or sister, baker, part-time worker, babysitter, gamer? All these different identities are important. Too few identities and you may stress too much over your sport, too many of these identities and you find it hard to give the time you need to your sport and may struggle to feel like you belong.

Activity: Typical–ideal day

Fill in the circles below as pie charts. Think about a typical day and all the things you have to do – school, homework, sports practice, sleeping, eating, travelling, playing games or watching TV, looking after brothers or sisters, part-time job, chatting to friends, music or art practice or other hobbies.

Then, in the second circle think about your ideal day – where would your split go? If you got to spend any time you wanted on anything you wanted what would you do?

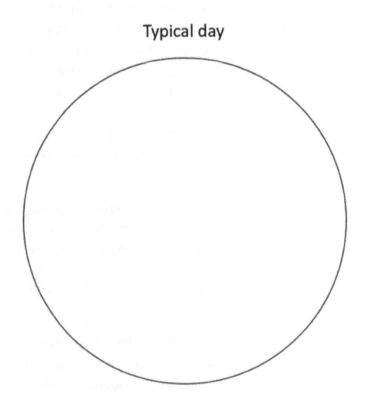

Typical day

Ideal day

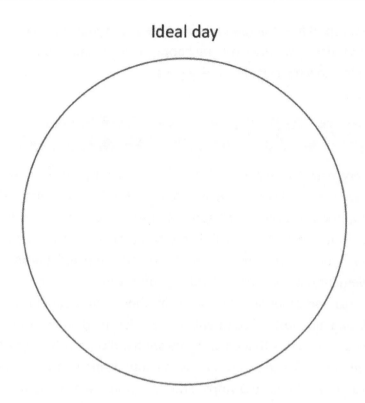

The charts you get should highlight what sits within your identity.

I am currently _____ % athlete. I would like to be _____% athlete.

If you are more athlete than you would like to be it is time to find fun stuff outside of sport. It means when you retire or have a setback or injury you will have friends around you who care about supporting you, not just excited by what you have achieved in sport. It means your whole day won't be made or lost by how well training is going – and sporting failures won't feel like personal failures.

If you are less of an athlete than you would like to be then some time spent thinking about how seriously you want to take your sport would be good and working through what is holding you back.

If your typical day and ideal day are pretty similar than happy days, you've got your balance right. In your case sport is simply one of the things you do – it is not who you are. Each time you achieve something with your sport it certainly adds to your life and to your enjoyment – but it doesn't dictate whether you are happy or sad. A bad result shouldn't determine how the rest of your day goes.

COMPARE – BUT ONLY WITH OURSELVES

It is very hard to keep our own sense of identity within our sport when we constantly get compared to others. It becomes about them and not about us. Almost all sport is designed around some sort of comparison. Our bodies (usually in pretty tight clothing) are on display, our performances are timed or measured and compared, tracking and achievement data gets posted online, and if you become high profile the media and other athletes may chat about your data in public, in detail, and not just in competition but also in training. There are rankings and ratings to look at. There are handicaps in Golf, Power of 10 in Athletics, Academy invitations in Football and Rugby and talent pathway offers in most Olympic and Paralympic sports. We all know where we sit compared to others of our age, in our area, in our club. Constant comparison. This is tough as an adult but as a teenager, when you are trying to get a handle on who you are, it is really hard. Don't beat yourself up for it – it is absolutely part of being a teen – but some of the activities here can make it a little less stressful to deal with.

Elite Insight: Siri Lindley (triathlon): In pre-race interviews I'd always get asked which athletes I had an extra close eye on going into the race. Without fail, I'd respond, 'I'm only worried about myself because I'm the only one I can control. All I can do is focus on myself and do my best every step of the way. The minute I start focusing on other athletes around me is the minute I start taking energy away from myself.' That answer served as an ongoing self reminder. It became my mantra.

Question: Do you look up your competitors before competing against them?

No ☐   Fantastic – carry on ignoring them.

Yes ☐   If it helps then carry on – but do it with purpose. Do it to study their competition style, the types of tactics they use and so you feel more knowledgeable and much better placed to compete against them.

Some of us thrive on knowing where we sit in the ranking. Others accept it for the way sport works. But it is a really bad way of helping us focus on ourselves.

We can't escape it a lot of the time. If you are on social media then you don't just get to constantly compare how fit you look or how hard you are training but how popular you are, how many friends you have, how many others you hang out with. We end up thinking everyone is happier, smarter, fitter; we think they have it all pulled together. They don't. They are just really good at impression management.

We are comparing their best Instagramed (Where they have taken 20 pictures to find a good shot) glossy views with our honest internal 'warts and all' ones. That image you have of someone else having it better is stage managed. We have to remind ourselves of that. While there is something oddly compelling about peering into the lives of others it can ruin our own motivation, so we are less likely to achieve our goals. It means the more we compare, the worse we are likely to do.

Our confidence will always be fragile if it depends upon how we do compared to others. We can't stop seeing what everyone else is up to but if we build our own confidence based on our own goals we can learn and master what matters to use so we feel more stable and in control. We can get used to comparing ourselves with ourselves. How were we doing 5 years ago, 3 years ago, last year? Have we got stronger, faster, higher? These are the comparisons worth doing. Then the glossy lives of others viewed through your phone no longer matter.

Activity: Completing a reality check

To do a reality check think about a professional athlete you admire. This activity will require some research into them; either google them or hunt out their autobiography or articles they have been mentioned in.

My favourite professional athlete is:

The three biggest setbacks they came up against were …

1.

2.

3.

The breakthroughs they have had in their career are …

1.

2.

3.

One way in which they are similar to me …

One way in which they are completely different to me …

This should highlight that we are all on our own sporting journey. We may have some things in common with other athletes but we'll have a lot different and so comparing ourselves with ourselves is a much more valuable route.

COPING WITH COMPARISON

If we do find ourselves either being compared with others either at an event or over social media perhaps take the same stance that Shaun Wright-Phillips talked about in Chapter 5: to only listen to the opinions of those who matter to you. He could ignore the media and the fans because he knew what was important was whether he carried out the wishes of his manager and was a great teammate to the other players. Beyond those people other opinions were simply opinions and not of relevance to him.

Activity: Circle of influence

Pick four people you trust and really value their opinion. This might be your parents or caregivers, coach, teammate or PE teacher. These will be the people to listen to and value. Tuning your ears into what they feed back to you about your performance and behaviours will help you tune out what is said by those whose opinions are irrelevant to your performance.

My circle of influence:

1.

2.

3.

4.

SHAPING THE CULTURE AND CLIMATE

With our self-identity sussed the other area of huge importance is the type of people and the culture that surrounds us in our sport. This culture will include the physical and mental environment that you train and play in and the way the people in that environment behave towards each other. It can have a big impact on how we feel about our sport and how good we are at it. If we worry we are being judged or laughed at by others we will hold back. We will never feel comfortable. And while we want to stretch our comfort zone to do amazing things we need something to stretch in the first place. We can think of that comfort zone as psychological safety.

Psychological safety is essential to be great in sport. It can be very lonely on a sports field, on a trampoline, on the swim deck, or out on the track, knowing there are hundreds of pairs of eyes on you. It is not surprising so many of us feel over activated and under threat at that moment. But when we feel safe because we know we are surrounded by people who have our back and care about us, whether or not we win, it is much easier to lower our activation level and switch instead into the challenge mindset.

A psychologically safe sporting culture means you feel like you can take a risk, or try something new without fear of negative consequences. It means you can be completely honest with those you work with and can be more agile and innovative, testing ideas without feelings like your spot on the team is jeopardized. You feel you have space to fail, without judgement. To create this psychologically safe culture it needs a caring environment which is inviting and supportive and you feel valued and respected.

Elite Insight: Jonny Wilkinson (rugby): It is the attitude which says I will do whatever I can to help you guys be your best. If every member of the team is pushing others to excel while also being propelled forward by the rest of the team, this will bring the best part of everyone to the fore.

Support doesn't just make you feel good and give you some psychological safety. It protects you from burnout and stress, increases your motivation and means you deal better with adversity. Those supporting you don't need to be formally 'in your team' or even be expert or people paid to give advice. In fact, while you will always want your coach or technical experts (physiologist, strength and conditioning, psychologist, nutritionist) to be a professional and usually paid to help you, most people – teachers, friends, parents, wider family, teammates or even people you know online – won't have a formal role but can still help you and be really effective. They can give the emotional support we need when putting our heart and soul into something really difficult. They can give us the space to vent feelings and get some reassurance so we feel less frantic when things are uncertain or stressful.

Activity: Support team identification

Write down here who is your 'go to' person for each issue (it is fine if the same person or people come up regularly).

Sporting advice	
Fitness advice	
Training advice	
Competition advice	
Nutrition advice	
Injury advice	
Health advice	
Psychological advice	

Family or relationship advice	
When I need cheering up	
When I need school advice	
When I want to have fun	
When I need to talk about something personal	

There are three specific groups of people who are likely to have come up a lot in your support team identification – family, coaches, friends and teammates. We'll look at how they help (and sometimes hinder) how well we can do and how to use them to help you perform at your very best.

SUPPORT FROM FAMILY

However seriously we take our sport we will always be a person first and an athlete second. This means we need to ensure our basic human needs are met – and one of those is connection to others. Even if you train incredibly hard, it is likely to be for up to a couple of hours a day. The rest of the time you are a regular teenager, trying to find your way through teenage life. Some of this time will be spent with your family. Some of this time might be spent trying to also get some independence. This can be challenging as you need your parents or caregivers to support you in your sport – especially for paying for classes or club fees, for travel to competitions and training and for giving comfort and reassurance when a big event is coming up, but also trying to develop some independence and ownership of your sport yourself.

On the one hand we need the support. Researchers have found it doesn't only make us feel better but it actually builds our confidence and improves our performance. When golfers were asked about support it was found that when those with strong social support systems were playing stressful matches they improved their golf score by one shot per round. The golfers without that system in place played worse.

On the other hand, if families get too involved it can cause problems. Too much focus on competition (rather than fun and practice and mastery) adds lots of additional and unhelpful pressure. Too much cheer-leading may give you a false impression of your true potential. Overly competitive parents means you end up being forced into comparing yourself against others – even if you know that will damage your performance.

> Elite Insight: Jonny Brownlee (triathlon): You need to love what you are doing if you are going to develop into a successful senior athlete. Others will drop away if they are being pushed into it by parents. To make it you have got to love training.

Athletes like golfer Tiger Woods and Tennis player Andre Agassi have both discussed how their parents were very focused on them becoming professional athletes. They didn't get to choose their goals, or even their sports. They were pushed into them and their motivation came from trying to keep their parents happy rather than because they loved their sport. They both became great athletes but many others will have also been through this tough upbringing and it won't have made it into professional sport and now feel resentful.

> Elite Insight: Charlie Hodgson (rugby): You see these parents who get heavily involved in what their children are doing and the fact they are reliving their own childhood through their children which for me is such a wrong way to go. My dad was never an expert in Rugby. He liked it. He enjoyed the experience of watching it and he was proud watching my games but he would never comment on my performance.

Your happiness is far more important than fulfilling a frustrated parent's ambition for you. If you are pushed into sport it will feel hard work and you are likely to feel stressed and get burnt out. Athletes who are happy with how their parents were involved in their sport growing up say their parents were involved, warm and supportive without dominating. How would you like your parents to support you?

Activity: Parent support

There are lots of things parents do which they think are helpful to your sport. You may find them helpful. You may not. Look through the list below and tick in the right column. Perhaps you can show this to your parents to help them see how they can help in all the right ways?

Parent actions	Helpful	Not helpful
Wanting to talk about your sports lots at home		
Offering technical advice		
Offering motivational advice		
Reminding you how much time and money they have invested in you and your sport		
Giving you feedback on the outcome of your events		
Giving you feedback on the attitudes you showed in your events		
Telling you they love you however you have done in your competition		
Watching you at competitions		
Asking difficult questions to your coach on your behalf		
Cheering loudly at competitions		
Coaching you from the sidelines in competition		
Setting you goals for your sport		
Feeding back to coaches about how you are feeling		
Telling you about their own experiences in sport		

COACHES

How well we get on with our coach is really important. It impacts our performance and how we feel about how good we are at our sport. They are the people who will work with you to develop the skills you will need to be a great athlete. They should help you realise where your strengths lie and do everything they can to help you use them. They should also be honest with you and feed back where your weaknesses may be and how they might be holding you back.

It isn't always easy to get on with your coach. They might have lots of athletes to support. They might have a different style of communication. And this is really critical as studies asking athletes how well they get on with their coach have found they actually care more about how the coach communicates with them than what skills they may learn from them.

> Elite Insight: Rebecca Adlington (swimming): Your coach plays such a crucial role it needs to be a two way street. There has got to be trust and communication and you have got to respect that they will have goals just as much as you do. That relationship is really really crucial. Work on that relationship all the time and get to know each other and then the communication will only get better and better.

When you get on, communicate well and feel able to ask questions it will improve your confidence and it will mean you develop faster, feel more motivated and enjoy your sport more. All these things mean you are likely to perform better. When you don't get on it can feel really stressful, your development and improvement is slower and you are more likely to drop out or get burnt out.

Question: What am I looking for in my coach?

There are 15 different elements of coaching below. Which five matter most to you?

- Someone with good ethics and morals ☐
- Someone who is focused on the long term ☐
- Someone who listens to my views ☐
- Someone who understands me ☐
- Someone who respects me ☐
- Someone I trust ☐

- Someone I can chat to ☐
- Someone who is honest with me ☐
- Someone who pushes me ☐
- Someone who is kind ☐
- Someone who gives me confidence ☐
- Someone who tells me what to do ☐
- Someone who makes sport fun ☐
- Someone who will make me successful ☐
- Someone who is very patient ☐

Even when you have a coach you enjoy working with, who has lots of the elements you ticked above there is always a chance that things can go wrong. In these times it is essential you are both able to communicate well so it doesn't stop you from focusing on what is important: your performance and your enjoyment.

> Kelly Smith (football): "She [Hope, her coach] cares about me more as a person than as a footballer. She said that to me at my lowest point. She also made me realise she wouldn't leave me to struggle through my problems on my own. ... Hope always told me that she would be there to catch me if I fell ... those words meant the world to me."

Activity: Choose your coach communication

A great way to ensure you are able to communicate well in a crisis is to have practised communicating well when things are going good. Having a chat with your coach about how you like to get feedback and information and to understand how they like to give it means you both feel on firmer ground. Things you might like to include depending on your preferences.

Area	Possibilities	My own version
Receiving instructions	"I like to understand why I am being asked to do something. It helps me focus on it if I can see how it helps me become a better athlete." "When you spend a long time explaining why we are doing something I switch off. I work better when I am just told what to do."	
Having difficult conversations	"I take those tough conversations better at the end of a session so I can go home and think about them afterwards. If you do it at the beginning I just get grumpy in training." "Please could we have those tough conversations as soon as I get to training so I can start making a difference straight away."	
If not engaging with sessions	"If I am not engaging well it isn't that I don't respect you or our sport but I am usually tired from school/feeling nervous that day/a bit overwhelmed with how much I have to learn and I tend to hide away."	
Giving feedback	"I really like blunt, honest feedback straight away that I can go away and work on." "I prefer to watch back videos of my events and pull out my own feedback and ask you how I work on that later."	
Motivation	"Before competition I like you to motivate me. Make me feel like I can achieve my goals." "Before competition I like you to give me instructions and advice. Tell me how to do it."	

FRIENDS AND TEAMMATES

The other really important group of supporters in sport are our friends and family. They help us do better, make training or practice more fun and help us feel like we can achieve more. There are lots of benefits of friends and teammates in sport:

- They can listen – and in a way that doesn't feel like we are being judged or having to take lots of advice.
- They can offer empathy – so we feel like someone is on our side.
- They can offer actual assistance – so they take things off our plate and make our lives easier.
- They make training more fun and effective – we are more likely to turn up to training when we know we have people we like hanging out with there. We also know we'll have a friendly face when we get to competitions.
- In team sports the team climate is much warmer when everyone gets on – less bitching, no gossiping about others, all working together for the same goal. And no one loafing – letting everyone else work hard and just hanging onto your coat tails.
- In individual sports having a training partner gives many of these benefits, in particular spurring each other on and even copying each other's techniques or attitudes so you both improve.
- In technical sports training with others means we can mirror and learn from each other.
- We even get better accountability when we train with others. Some researchers studied the role of spotters for those doing the bench press. When lifters thought spotters were watching them they are able to do more reps and reported that the reps felt easier.

The support doesn't have to be from current friends or teammates. To find your 'tribe' you might have to go further afield. That might be on training days if you are in a smaller sport or on a talent pathway or even online into forums for your sport.

Elite Insight: Alistair Brownlee (triathlon): Even at our level it is so much easier training hard and well when you are doing it with someone else. If I know I can meet a friend at the track to do a hard session together it makes it seem possible.

Activity: What kind of teammate or training partner do I want to be?

There are lots of ways to be a great teammate – and to be a dreadful one. Look at the behaviours below and tick three that you will aim to follow to be a teammate you are proud of:

Helpful to others ☐

Supportive towards others ☐

Assists the coaches (with equipment, etc.) ☐

Cuts down any gossiping I hear ☐

Welcoming any new members ☐

Offers advice to others ☐

Puts in full effort to every session ☐

Asks others for feedback ☐

Listens to instructions ☐

Is approachable ☐

Gives others confidence ☐

One of the great benefits of feeling confident in who we are and having people on our side is that when it comes to competition we have lots of people cheering us on. Some online, or in mind, others physically there with you. These cheers are powerful and effective.

The cheers don't need to be loud and in your ear during your event. They can be statements given in training beforehand, comments made in feedback conversations, nuggets of advice in team talks or a motivational quote offered. They help your confidence to know that someone else truly believes you have the ability and effort levels to achieve your goals. The fact someone has taken some time out of their day to give you their encouragement is another boost.

The statements they make when they cheer might focus on your main strengths, technical points (as long as this won't annoy you) or a reminder that you have the skills and experiences that are needed to do well. You want it to feel authentic. Your brain is far too clever to accept fake news – you see straight through it.

When the four rules of cheering are followed it can work really well:

1. It needs to come from someone who actually knows what they are talking about so it is authentic.
2. It needs to come from someone you trust.
3. Any statements should be based on facts – it has to be believable.
4. What is said should link to your skills or experiences.

Question: What do you like your supporters to cheer?

STARTING TRICKY CONVERSATIONS

There will be times where we need to have difficult conversations with either our parents or our coach. Planning for these takes away some of the nerves we might have about them and helps you feel a little bit more in control of the situation.

Some athletes are just happy to go along with whatever their coach or parents plan. Others like to understand why they are doing something: What is the purpose? How will it help them perform better? Asking these things isn't being difficult or disrespectful but helping you learn more about your sport and how to be good at it.

You need this communication to respond in the best way. For example, if you suddenly find yourself dropped from the first team to the reserves and don't know why, it could hugely dent your motivation. If you get brave enough to ask, you might find the coaches tell you that they needed a strong athlete in the reserves to give weaker athletes a mentor or that they don't think you have been focused well enough recently to stay in the first team. Both answers give you a greater understanding of the situation.

Some things to remember when you have to have a tricky conversation:

1. It can be good to give a heads-up before the conversation by saying that you have something to talk about and you would value some time with them – this makes them realise you are serious and open to chat – not just angry and going to shout at them.

2. Both of you will have your own versions of the truth and the way you see things. That is ok. The conversation is there to help you see each other's viewpoint and find a way to move forward.

3. Try not to sit face to face – it can feel a bit like you might fight. The nicest way to have a tricky chat is to walk side by side with someone. If you want to have that chat with your parents then doing it sitting in the front of the car on a trip to training can work well too as it feels less emotional.

4. Think about what you want from the conversation. This helps us stress less about the small stuff we may have to suck up in order to get the thing which is most important to us. It can help to write this down beforehand so you can read it if you get flustered.

5. However frustrating it may be, really listening to the other side of the conversation so you can answer their concerns – not just throw in your points (which is always incredibly tempting) – means you'll learn more, understand their viewpoint better and not feel you are going round in circles.

6. Make sure you have enough time to chat. Getting interrupted by other athletes or your siblings can undo all the bravery of having the conversation in the first place.

7. Summarise your chat with what you will do as a result of it, what you understand the other person will do and when you will next check in with them.

SUCCESS STORY: MARILYN OKORO

Marilyn Okoro is a British 400- and 800-metre runner. She has been winning medals on the international stage since 2007 and her medal drawer holds an Olympic Bronze, World Bronze and a European Silver. She is still training.

> I always say I am more than just an athlete. Always. At school I was in the Lacrosse Team and in the Debate team and in the Choir and I had strong bonds with my friends and I was close to my family so there is so much more to be than just being an athlete. It definitely helped me in the beginning as an athlete to have that balance. It helped me not burn out.
>
> When I was racing when young I wasn't 100% focused on me but I also wasn't focused on the other girls either. I think I was focused on what other people's expectations were and being so desperate to prove that I could deliver. A lot of my race anxiety was to do with thinking "you can't mess this up because everyone is expecting you to mess this up." Some days you do mess it up because that dominating thought takes over but some days I got it amazingly right.

Much of the time in my career I think I was not really running on my terms and not really understanding what I was doing. I was always expecting to be told. I was looking a lot to my coaches for guidance but I've had lots of different coaches so that means I've had lots of different ideologies and different training systems. I wasn't really encouraged to ask questions or understand what I was doing I was just told "this is how you run fast." It meant I wasn't learning anything. Questioning is so important. They were telling me what I was doing wrong but not how to correct it and they were focusing on what I wasn't good at a lot of the time and I wasn't getting a lot of praise. I really do need that praise in my training, even now.

Throughout much of my career I didn't have a mentor and I think that is why I want to mentor now. I had these people to look up to but I didn't know how to access them. Remotely I learnt a lot from Serena Williams. She is not afraid to be herself and express her emotions and I want to be the same and be able to be my authentic self. I felt I could resonate with her and learn a lot about how to conduct myself.

At times I felt extremely lonely. I was in an environment where it was almost encouraged to keep pushing yourself and no-one tells you when to pull back and when to stay on the safe side. There is a very big culture of just smash everything and that becomes a bit dangerous. That is where having a mentor comes in and they can look out for your welfare. Especially in youngsters – helping you to know it is ok to just hold back and enjoy it and build the consistencies. You need to learn things about yourself and learn how your body responds to different stimuluses. You also need to learn that when you go to major championships you are in the form of your life and you are not going to run every round with PBs so you need to learn to conserve and use your energy wisely otherwise in the long run you will pay for it with burnout or injury.

I think it is really important to find the right coach. I have made some interesting choices because I wasn't researching enough who I was asking to coach me and who I was putting all my trust in. How they communicate their ideologies and theories is very important but they might also need to be ok to chuck some of that out the window if things don't add up.

I've been in some amazing groups and communities. Everyone talks about team GB but we are only Team GB when we are picked for the championship we are going to. Until that point you are in your silos in your little training groups. They are like your immediate family in sport and they see you in your good sessions and your bad sessions. The most effective training group I've been in was one where we had lots of different events; sprints to cross country and for me being such a combination athlete it worked because on different days I always had someone I could run with. I really do value the importance of having a good community around me but I always think it starts with the coach leading that culture and setting the tone for how everyone relates to each other.

CHAPTER 9

I can feel like an athlete

If you practise your sport every day for an hour that is 7 hours a week or 365 hours a year. Then add on all the time you spend getting to practise, around competitions, doing fitness or strength work and you could easily be over 500 hours a year. Do you want to spend 500 hours a year uncomfortable, pretending to be something or someone you are not? Or do you want to feel 100% you when training, fully relaxed and most able to perform at your best?

We can read lots of books or listen to interviews to understand how medallists and champions managed to achieve their excellence in sport; you will have read the Elite Insights and interviews in this book, but you have your own journey. Other athletes' stories will give you an idea of what it is like to compete in sport at a high level but when you get there you will be following your own path. You need to feel comfortable with who you are as an athlete. To do this we need to feel secure in what matters to us, why our sport is important and how we perform best. When we really understand ourselves and become aware of how we think and feel and when we understand our preferences and our personalities, we can behave in a way that matches that. This really helps us get through tough times as it helps us develop and understand our purpose.

In Chapter 8 we looked at the different self-identities we might have as a teenager and how much of our identity is as an athlete. How much we feel like an athlete is important as it shapes the attitude we use in training and competition, how well we look after our body and wellbeing and how professionally we approach what we do. And we don't just want to feel like an athlete but a professional one – understanding brilliantly our sport, our bodies and ourselves. This is what we will focus on in this final chapter.

PURPOSE + PASSION = PERFORMANCE

Sport can be brilliant fun, but some days it can be really hard. If it was easy we wouldn't be developing and improving; we wouldn't get the satisfaction when we succeed. So the difficulty is important, but what is equally important is knowing why we do it. What drives us: something inside ourselves (the love of the movement) or what we get from doing well in it (the prizes, respect from others, the social life).

When we really love our sport we enjoy it more. We spend the time we are physically doing it feeling good and the time around it hanging out with great friends. So we need to understand our purpose: Why do we do our sport?

Our purpose and passions for sport will all be different. We can think of ourselves like a cake. The ingredients are our personality traits, the way we have been brought up, what we have done previously and what matters to us as a person. The baking process is impacted by where we train, who trains us, the ambitions we have. The decoration comes from the skills we learn and the mental processes we develop to pull everything together to perform under pressure in competition. When we understand how all these elements add different flavours and what our personal 'recipe' is, then we can use this knowledge to our advantage. We can look to two areas to go shopping for our basic ingredients: motivation and values.

Motivation

A key part of our cake recipe comes down to our type of motivation. We discussed this in Chapter 3 but it is so important that it is worth a reminder. There are three types: amotivation, extrinsic and intrinsic.

Amotivation describes itself. I don't care and I can't be bothered. It is the sporting version of 'meh'. You may have mixed all the ingredients together but it is like putting the cake mix in the oven without turning it on. It won't change into something edible or able to be decorated.

Extrinsic motivation is when we are playing our sport for reasons that are outside of ourselves – to win medals, awards or prize money, to see our friends, to be accepted by a group we want to be part of, to keep our parents happy. This can work well and you can bake a great cake – but it might not be decorated in just the way you'd like it or taste the way you want it. It will always be driven by something or someone else and that takes away a bit of our power. It means if we suffer a setback, like not being picked for an event or getting an injury, we might really struggle to get back into sport and do the hard grind that is necessary. You can do well for a while but once you reach higher levels and it takes longer and longer to step up to the next rung on the ladder and you are competing against people just as good as you then enthusiasm will be really hard to come by and sport will just feel like yet another chore you have to complete.

Ideally, you will have intrinsic motivation. This comes when we do our sport because we love it. We love the feeling of the movements in our bodies, the sense of achievement afterwards, the passion for learning new skills and mastering them. This type of motivation carries on even if we are performing awfully because it is not about results or rewards but simply getting to be active and do the process we love. With intrinsic motivation we don't just have the purpose to do our sport we have passion to – and if you mix these two together you bake a 'bake off' winning cake.

Elite Insight: Laura Kenny (cycling): I get asked about being an inspiration to young girls. Well, I still feel exactly like the eight-year old kid who raced because she loved it. I didn't want fame for this. I didn't want money from it and I didn't want admiration. I just did it because bike riding is my life.

Activity: Pick your purpose

To understand which type of motivation you have and what is your purpose for competing in your sport you need some free time and some space to think. Free writing can help you do this. Read through the questions below and then simply jot down all your reasons for doing your sport. Paragraphs, bullet points or just words; it doesn't matter just get everything down on paper.

I compete in my sport because …

Look back over your words. Can you circle any extrinsic reasons (trophies, medals, praise, future career options) and put a square around the intrinsic motivations (feelings, thoughts, processes)? Think about how you could focus more on the elements in squares and less on the ones which are circled.

Some of the things you may have squared or circled:

If you are intrinsically motivated ...	If you are extrinsically motivated ...
My sport is fun	My sport is good for me
I feel good when I do my sport	I love doing well in my sport
I enjoy training for my sport	I enjoy competing in my sport
I enjoy learning new sports skills	I have to focus hard in my sport to do well
I choose to do my sport	I like the rewards of my sport

If there were lots of intrinsic motivation squares you may naturally love your sport and so will stick with it, whatever obstacles get in your way. If there were lots more of circles you may not have a natural love for your sport so we need to find ways to manipulate our motivation. We can firstly amp up any squares so we can. Use any intrinsic motivation to get out and be active and then boost it with external rewards. The stronger these rewards are (often having exciting goals) the better able we are to keep going even when we have that loud devil on our shoulder telling us to stop.

Values

There is more to our purpose though than just our motivation. There are also our values. We don't often talk about values and it is rare you would be asked what they are but knowing yours helps you make choices so you spend your time and effort on the things which matter to you. They really help you develop your own independent thought. When you are able to live by your values and make your own choices in line with them your chance of being intrinsically motivated rises. When your values and actions line up you can put so much more passion into your performances. Then you have the power to be a fantastic athlete.

Values are incredibly helpful when you find yourself comparing your-self and judging your self-worth through the usual sporting metrics: I lost a match, I didn't get a new personal best. What we can measure our-self against instead is whether we lived our values when playing sport. Many of the young athletes I work with have fairness as a core value. Instead of judging a match purely on the score, a tennis player might judge their match on whether they made any dubious line calls or called out an opponent doing so. Another core value many have is family so instead of judging their competition on whether they got a medal they can judge it through whether they made their parents proud through their effort levels and sportspersonship. Then they feel truly successful.

Our values really drive who we are at our deepest level and start to come to life as we become teenagers. If we are able to start living by them then we will feel much more in control of everything going on around us.

Values also help us to stay more in line with our ethics in sports. How would you deal with a squash player dragging out the time between serves, someone cutting the corner in cross-country or a rider sitting too close behind you in a cycling time trial? When you are sure of your own values you can feel more secure with how you respond to any of these issues. When we get to elite levels these values become even more important. Too often we have heard of athletes in teams being pressured into taking performance-enhancing drugs because that is just 'what everyone does'. Knowing whether those behaviours match our values helps us decide how to respond to those pressures. It is much easier to tackle things which feel unethical when we are basing our response on who we feel we truly are.

Your values can also help you pick the right team or coach to work with. If your values are around openness, creativity and humour then working with an old school coach who doesn't like to be questioned and expects 100% quiet and focus during sessions is probably not going to feel fun to work with. But, if your values were around dedication, deci-siveness and strength, then they might be ideal for you.

Activity: Find your values

On this page are 50 different values. Consider what each means to you. We would like you to cross off all those which you don't immediately go 'Yes – that is me.' It should be easy to cross off about 25 of them. Then it gets much harder. Ideally, we would like you to get down to no more than five values. These will be your core values.

Achievement	Family	Loyalty
Affection	Flexibility	Mastery
Ambition	Forgiveness	Open-minded
Bravery	Freedom	Optimistic
Competition	Friendship	Positivity
Control	Gratitude	Pride
Creativity	Growth	Productivity
Curiosity	Happiness	Quality
Adventurousness	Harmony	Recognition
Decisiveness	Health	Respect
Dependability	Humour	Security
Discipline	Independence	Strength
Efficiency	Innovation	Teamwork
Empathy	Integrity	Trust and honesty
Equality	Intelligence	Variety
Excitement	Kindness	Rich
Spiritual	Love	Wisdom

When we have highlighted our few core values we can recognise ourselves much better and tie those into our sport so we can perform much better.

SELF-EXPERT

Elite athletes learn to not just be an expert in their sport, but also an expert in themselves. While performance analysts will break down what you do in your sport into numbers (and numbers are great because they are clear and easy to work on) you are more than a bunch of numbers. Much more. You need to analyse yourself to feel really comfortable that you are making the most of who you are in your sport. And no one knows you better than you. If you can become really self-aware of your likes, dislikes, fears, strengths, weaknesses, training and recovery preferences then you can design and adapt your training and competition environments to really work for you so you maximise enjoyment and minimise the stresses.

> Elite Insight: Rebecca Adlington (swimming): Believe in yourself and stick to your gut. I think your instincts and your gut as an athlete take you so far and I think you have to know yourself what works for you and trust in that. You have got to know yourself inside and out.

There are three P's of becoming a self-expert: perception, personality and preferences.

Perceptions

One way to really get to know yourself while training is to actually record yourself while training. Best do this when training alone but the idea is you literally say out loud the things you are thinking in your head while training with your voice being recorded on your phone. It helps you notice what you think about and what type of thoughts are running through your head. You'll be able to see where your attention and focus goes. You can see what distracts you – and what gets you excited. Listening back to your recording afterwards will help you identify themes of things you think about. The technique is called 'Think Aloud'. Obviously there is a caveat that this doesn't work if your sport involves being in the water or flying through the air!

Activity: Thinking aloud

Do a regular training session but every time you think about something say it out loud into the Dictaphone on your phone. Depending on the sport you do you might be able to have headphones in so you are talking into a mic or you may have to talk louder than usual.

After your session sit down with this page, listen to your recording and write down:

Things I mention a lot?

Things I found hard?

Things I was surprised I didn't mention?

Thoughts that were unhelpful to my practice?

As part of the 'getting to know' ourselves process we need to understand not just 'how' things are but how we 'think' they are. When we really focus on what we think about we are better able to monitor our own mind. This really helps our performances in sport as we can control unhelpful thoughts or behaviours better and emphasise the elements which help us master our sport.

The processes we use to understand how we think about sport actually help us cope under pressure. In competition, when our brains sometimes feel overloaded with too much information, the athletes who really know themselves and the potential impact of behaviours or moves on their mindset will be able to work much more efficiently so they can perform at a higher level. They will be much more aware of which mental skills to use and more aware of what they don't yet know so they can spend some time and effort improving in those areas.

Questions: Thinking about ourselves

How often do you go back to your process goals and think about whether you are following them?

How many questions do you ask yourself in your training diary?

How often do you catch yourself thinking 'unhelpful' thoughts?

What will you do as a result of these answers?

Personality

Our personality is our own personal pattern of feeling, thinking and behaving. Studies have found that our personality can impact our happiness, health, relationships and how well we work with others. It can also influence how successful we are likely to be in our sport.

In sport some of our success will be directed by our ability to cope with pressure and willingness to use effort and persevere; we can look at which personality traits help us do that. The traits we often study are neuroticism (how prone you are to emotional instability), extraversion (how much we thrive and get our energy from being around other people), openness (how much we look for new experiences), agreeableness (how much we seek cooperation and social harmony) and conscientiousness (how much we organise and direct our efforts towards our goals).

If you compare elite athletes to regular people or even amateur athletes, they tend to:

- Be more extroverted (become energised by the competition environment and happy to stick to plans with a social element)
- Have lower levels of neuroticism (so more emotionally stable in competition)
- Be highly conscientious (so they prepare for competition really well)
- Have high levels of agreeableness (can get on with coach and teammates)
- Have higher levels of openness (up for trying new things)

These don't tend to predict how well you will do in a single event as there are so many elements which can alter the outcome of an event but they do hold over time with studies on junior athletes being able to predict from their personality profiles whether they have a higher chance of making it in elite sport.

Studies have also found that athletes with low levels of agreeableness and extraversion are more likely to behave aggressively and those with low levels of openness and high neuroticism are more likely to use coping strategies which see them avoid competition or stressful situations. Athletes with high levels of conscientiousness, extraversion and low neuroticism are much more likely to use the problem-focused coping strategies which have been found to be most effective.

Interestingly, if you have high levels of extroversion you should outperform introverts (the opposite of extroverts) when you have an audience or supporters but without that audience there should not be much difference. The extroverts can also benefit from being angry when they compete too as it seems to up their levels of performance.

A final point from the research in this area is that when you are looking to hire a coach or choose between teams to join it is worth looking at how they display extroversion and openness. Ideally you want their levels on each to match yours. If you and your coach are opposites on these traits you might find it difficult to work together.

So, what does this all mean if we don't match the 'ideal personality' for an elite athlete? It doesn't mean you can't make it or you should give up. Just that you'll need to be aware where these traits might make it a bit harder for you so you will need to practise a lot of the techniques in this book, so you have the mental skills in place to be braver, more flexible and emotionally more stable.

Preferences

Now that you have an understanding of what you think about your sport it is next important to understand what you prefer within your sport. How do our preferences make us behave? If we can become an authority on ourselves we can become far more self-aware of our likes, dislikes, preferences and fears. This helps us to design or adapt competition environments to maximise enjoyment and potential success.

Elite Insight: Mo Farah (running): There's a fine line. The more you race, the more you begin to understand your body and how it responds to different approaches to training. What works for somebody else doesn't necessarily work for you.

None of these preferences in themselves have a negative or positive impact on how well we perform but if we are forced into following a route that doesn't suit our preference we may well feel uncomfortable, more anxious, over activated, stressed or pushed into a threat mindset. In this way understanding what we like and aiming to follow it has great benefits.

Activity: Preference checklist

There are an infinite amount of preferences we could have, but some really important ones for athletes are covered here:

Training and sports practice

I prefer to train with others ☐

I prefer to train on my own ☐

I am happy to train alone or with others ☐

Before competitions

I like to chat to other competitors or teammates ☐

I like to be alone and in my own space ☐

Happy to take or leave other people ☐

Advice

Love to get advice from my coach ☐

Love to get advice from my parents ☐

No advice please – want to be left alone ☐

Logistics

   I like to plan everything and arrive with plenty of time ☐

   I leave the organisation to others ☐

   I hate waiting around – I turn up just before the start ☐

Nutrition

My go-to food on the morning of a competition is …

My favourite drink to have in competition is …

Just before we start an event I like to eat …

Competition struggles

   I focus on making my head chatter more positive ☐

   I use my motivational mantra ☐

   I do some colourful breathing ☐

   I focus on my goal ☐

   I use Respond, React, Relax and Refocus ☐

To get my nerves to the right level before a competition I use:

   Music ☐

   Chatting to others ☐

   Deep breathing ☐

   Imagery ☐

   Helpful head chatter ☐

   Following my pre-performance routine ☐

Avoiding nervous looking people ☐

Warming up really well ☐

Injury

If I get injured I want to hide away from my sport ☐

I learn everything I can about my injury ☐

I find lots of ways to fill the time ☐

I still go to training so I don't miss out ☐

I do all my rehab exercises ☐

WELLBEING

Finally, we will never perform brilliantly as an athlete if we don't look after our bodies and our brains. This isn't about following the latest research on wearing compression tights, sitting in ice-baths or drinking beetroot juice but on making yourself strong and healthy, both physically and mentally.

To feel good and able to take on competition in sport and to be able to behave as a professional athlete we need a number of layers in place: feeling physically safe, healthy, part of a group, having confidence in yourself and then working towards something which matters for you. We need to feel like we have got a good balance between skills we can already do and skills which challenge and stretch us. With these in place we can get into the right mindset for sport where we can be completely absorbed and enjoy playing or competing.

For all of these layers we need to feel secure. There was an American psychologist in the 1940s, Abraham Maslow, who devised a model called the Hierarchy of Needs. Much of it still makes sense today. It looks like a pyramid, with the most crucial needs at the bottom, and says only when each layer is in place do we start to benefit from the next layer.

Layer 1: The bottom layer is physiological safety. Here we need to know that our main physical requirements for survival – food, water, sleep and shelter – are all in place. We will never be able to perform well in competition if we are worried about whether we had somewhere to go back to afterwards.

Layer 2: The next layer is safety. This relates to our physical, personal, emotional, financial and health. If we are unwell we can't compete. If we have no money for entry fees we can't compete. That security is needed to allow us to attempt excellence. Without these things we can never reach our potential.

Layer 3: This level is about social belonging – our need to have family and friendships. It is that need to belong to something bigger than ourselves. This helps us get that feeling of psychological safety we discussed in the last chapter. When we have achieved this layer we feel comfortable enough to be vulnerable, to be honest and to express our true opinions, without fear of getting told off or asked to pipe down.

Layer 4: This is where we need to value and respect ourselves. And this is the layer many athletes get stuck on. They may have everything else in place but with low confidence and a feeling that our self-esteem is always under threat then we will struggle to perform at our absolute best and have in place all we need to achieve that feeling of flow when it feels like everything has come together.

Layer 5: This layer is what we are striving for. When it all comes together and we have that feeling of flow when we feel like we are within touching distance of our potential and we get lost in the moment. This will mirror intrinsic motivation where you find yourself in your sport purely for the love of it – of the movement and the feelings. When we hit flow we can feel like we are in the zone. It is what many athletes play for – those moments when it all comes together and you feel like you are flying. No one has yet found a guaranteed route to flow but the more you have these first four layers in place the more likely it is to arrive. When you add in the ideas we have discussed on following the process and focusing on the 'now' rather than the outcome or the future then you can use your overall well-being to enhance your sports performance.

Elite Insight: Laura Kenny (cycling): Being in the zone for me is being on my bike, on the track, and it all feeling effortless. The riding, the tactics, the timing, the big moves. All of it without thinking, all of it without consciously trying.

SLEEP

Of all those elements in the pyramid one I feel every teenage athlete will benefit from a better quality sleep. Sleep is often the first thing to go when we feel stressed and overwhelmed with how much we have to do in life as a teenage athlete. When we don't get enough sleep it really messes with us.

Sleep improves your school performance (as it is when you consolidate the learning you have done each day) and improves your sporting performance (as it is when your body recovers and gets stronger). When Stanford University asked their swim team to spend at least 10 hours in bed each night their speeds, tumble turns and reaction times all improved. It also means you reduce your risk of injury or infection which can prevent you from training. A study of teenage athletes in California found that those who slept fewer than 8 hours a night were 1.7 times more likely to have an injury.

We all have our own sleep needs so you may be different but UCL, a university that does lots of research in this area, suggests that teenage athletes need around 9 hours of sleep a night.

Getting to know our sleep patterns and our biological clock is really helpful to help us train at the right times and to get to sleep fairly quickly so we don't lie awake getting annoyed that you can't sleep. School doesn't help this though. Most teenagers' brains work as owls (liking to go to sleep late and get up late) and do so until their early 20s. It means you function better in the evening and don't feel tired until really late. If you have to get up early for school or training then you'll miss out on lots of sleep. You need to learn some tricks to help you get to sleep earlier. One of these is really knowing your circadian rhythm.

Your circadian rhythm is your body's natural cycle that sets out when you will fall asleep, feel hungry, thirsty, feel tired or alert and be able to focus. Each cycle is about 90 minutes long and in that time we will have one peak and one dip. If we understand when our peaks and dips are we can use them to become better athletes.

Firstly, knowing your peaks and troughs can help explain poor performance (if we are competing during our dip) so we can be a bit kinder to ourselves. If we know we have a dip coming in a training session we can do a different part of our training over that period and adjust our approach and do harder stuff 45 minutes later when we will peak.

Secondly, it is good to know that when we are in a dip we might be more vulnerable. Our brain feels tired so we are more likely to make rash decisions or eat unhealthy foods or make poor choices. If we are tempted to do something which will harm our ability to be great in sport then waiting just 15 minutes until we are out of the dip can tell us if we really want to do that thing or if it was just a self-destructive craving caused by our circadian rhythm.

Finally, knowing when we dip means we can go to bed at the right time, just before a dip. If we go to bed after our dip we'll have to wait nearly 90 minutes before we are likely to feel tired again and might well get frustrated knowing we've lost over an hour's sleep. To learn when our dips come we have to get yawn spotting.

Activity: Yawn spotting

We all yawn multiple times a day (often after lunch, and especially in the evening when we're tired). Each time you yawn, jot down the time. Over a few days you'll start to see a pattern and there should be around 90 minutes between each set of yawns. Then you can add 90 minutes onto each set and see when your 16 dips will be each day. Add 45 minutes to these and you have your peaks.

Date	Yawn 1	Yawn 2	Yawn 3	Yawn 4

My morning dips (so a good time to do easier activities):

My evening dips (a good time to go to bed):

My morning peaks (a good time to train hard):

My afternoon peaks (a good time to study or train hard):

SUCCESS STORY: RICHARD KRUSE

Richard Kruse is Britain's most successful Fencer. He won his first international medal at the 2001 European Under 20 Championships and is still winning medals at the highest level almost 20 years later. He has been to four Olympics, won gold in the GB team at the first ever European Games in 2015 and in 2019 achieved world number one ranking, the first British fencer to achieve that position. He shares with us how he navigates the life of an athlete.

There were three clear steps in my progression. I went from doing it once a week on a Saturday afternoon where it was just a hobby, just like you would go to a community club or a football club, to fencing while doing university and getting some results, to the transition of having it as a full time career. The results and the funding came at the right time to head in that direction and I committed to it fully.

One of the good things about my career was that the aim was the World and Olympics medal. I never got the Olympic medal but got the World Championships medal in 2018. The fact I was always chasing something that I never got till the very end actually helped me stay motivated.

I am motivated by fencing. I love the fencing. You have to love the game to be in it this long but if I was never able to win a match in fencing it would be a terrible sport for me so I think the fact I am good at something that I have an ability to win actually brings the enjoyment to the game itself. If I was never able to win it probably wouldn't be my sport.

When results came we celebrated them. We didn't dwell on them too much but we did mark good results but then we always moved forward pretty quickly to concentrate on the next thing.

I see the Fencers who are willing to challenge authority are the ones that seem to have a good personality for fencing. They see the World Champion and they want to go up and see how far they can push their luck and I think that kind of attitude, of wanting to push your limits, is good in sport. Not being intimidating but wanting to see how far you can go. Some people will be fencing in the Olympics and will think do I have the right to be in this match? Am I good enough to be here? Those with the challenging mindset wouldn't question it at all – they would just be there going for it.

I have quite an addictive personality. Being an elite level sportsman you get the endorphins, the adrenaline going into competitions and, when you win, the rush of endorphins can get quite addictive. I think that helped me quite a lot but it can be a big danger. I have seen some athletes go to some quite dark places and get involved with drugs, or alcohol or gambling because they have had this addiction to sport and the endorphins and when they are not getting that any more they try to find it elsewhere.

Your wellbeing can suffer a bit as a sportsman – especially if you overtrain. I think most athletes will have overtrained at some point in the pursuit of achieving more and more. When you go through that process you can get a bit demoralized, especially if you don't know what you are going through. And you can suffer from a bit of chronic fatigue of the nervous system. This has happened to me a few times. I remember in 2009 I won a competition in Copenhagen (so won six matches), two weeks later I was second in another competition so (won five matches) and two weeks later won another six matches to win another competition. I felt like I'd been knocked down. You have to rest that system to get back to normal.

Overtraining can have a real effect on your psychology. You can easily see the people who overtrain. They get a little bit withdrawn. A little bit depressed. When we used to train at Lee Valley one guy came from South London which was a five hour round trip. After a year he got fed up so his dad bought him a mobile home to stay in just over the road in the camp site. As a result he had a lot more free time so he started doing extra sessions, like an extra gym session every day. After a few months he really made himself quite ill because of over training. You then need a little bit of time away from the sport to recuperate.

My advice to young athletes would be to keep data on yourself with regards to training and really plan your year's schedule ahead of time. Then if you fall into any pitfalls and overtrain you have a record of what you have done so you can try and rectify that the following year.

Further reading

BBC. (2018). *Andy Murray Column: Why My Queen's Comeback against Kyrgios was So Emotional'*. https://www.bbc.co.uk/sport/tennis/44546047.

Bishop, C. (2020). *The Long Win*. Practical Inspirational Publishing.

Brownlee, A., & Brownlee, J. (2013). *Swim, Bike, Run: Our Triathlon Story*. Penguin UK.

Farah, M. (2016). *Twin Ambitions*. Hodder.

Grey-Thompson, T. (2020). *Recovery Summit*. 15th June 2020.

Holmes, K. (2005). *Black, White & Gold*. Virgin Books.

Johnson, M. (2012). *Gold Rush*. Harper Sport.

Kastor, D. (2018). *Let Your Mind Run*. Crown Archetype.

Lindley, S. (2016). *Surfacing*. VeloPress.

Nadal, R. (2012). *Rafa*. JC Lattès.

Nyad, D. (2015). *Find a Way*. Deckle Edge.

O'Sullivan, R. (2014). *Running*. Orion.

Palmer-Green, D., & Elliott, N. (2015). Sports injury and illness epidemiology: Great Britain Olympic Team surveillance during the Sochi 2014 winter Olympic games. *British Journal of Sports Medicine*, 49(1), 25–29.

Peters, S. (2013). *The Chimp Paradox: The Mind Management Program to Help You Achieve Success, Confidence, and Happiness*. TarcherPerigee.

Phelps, M., & Abrahamson, A. (2008). *No Limits: The Will to Succeed*. Simon and Schuster.

Rousey, R. (2015). *My Fight Your Fight*. Penguin.

Smith, K. (2013). *Footballer: My Story*. Corgi.

Spedding, C. (2011). *From Last to First: How I Became a Marathon Champion*. Aurum Press.

Spencer, C. (2020). *Mud, Maul, Mascara*. Unbound.

Steadman, L. (2020). *Recovery Summit*. 18th June 2020.

Trott, L. & Kenny, J. (2016). *The Inside Track*. Michael O'Mara.

Webber, M. (2015). *Aussie Grit: My Formula One Journey*. Pan Macmillan.

Wilkinson, J. (2009). *Tackling Life*. Headline.

Ten Top Tips

We asked the elite athletes interviewed in this book for what they would like you, as teenage athletes, to remember so you do well in your sport. Here is a selection of their great advice:

1. "As long as you're learning, you are making progress. Whatever the results, wherever you are in the rankings, whatever you know you still lack, as long as you can try to do something better today than last time, you are doing brilliantly." Cath Bishop

2. "Enjoy it – you have got to love your sport. If you love the game you are always going to work hard and learn." Shaun Wright-Phillips

3. "Be prepared – don't try and wing it. It is the winging it which gives you the anxiety. The more prepared you are the more in control you are and that helps reduce those feelings of anxiety." Charlie Hodgson

4. "See the opportunity in any situation. Look for the opportunities which will help you towards that end goal." Emma Wiggs

5. "Reach out and talk with people. So many older athletes want to help. They have invaluable experience that you just won't find from anyone else and can be really helpful at any point in your career." Rebecca Adlington

6. Your coach plays such a crucial role; it needs to be a two-way street of trust and communication. Once you see each other as human beings not just as athlete and coach the respect is better and you have communication and openness of what you are both trying to achieve." Becky Adlington

7. "Take every opportunity to ask questions, to learn and to review everything about your game and your sport. Seek questions from coaches. Seek questions from senior players; what do I need to improve on? What do I need to do well? Be in a constant 'do and review' phase." Joe Weatherly

8. "Keep a training diary. It is discipline. You can learn so much from looking back in your training diary." Marilyn Okoro

9. "Give yourself space to breathe – I think sometimes young athletes want it to happen too fast or think it should be changing too quickly and actually if it is worth doing, it is worth waiting for." Dame Sarah Storey

10. "Elite level sport doesn't equate to an easy life. About a quarter of the year you will have these James Bond moments where you are going round the world and will be winning tournaments in weird places. Living the high life. But three quarters of the year is head down training." Richard Kruse